SURVIVAL TIPS

AND

TACTICS

Natural Disaster Survival Guide

Conrad Blake

Survival Prepping Guides Series

ISBN-13: 978-1530592586

ISBN-10: 1530592585

Table of Contents

To my father, my hero
and bushcraft enthusiast

WHEN DISASTER STRIKES

A word to the wise: knowing basic survival skills is one thing, using them is another. If you do not practice these skills, and become proficient at them, this book will be of little use to you. Gaining this knowledge is a good start, but if you have never experienced its practical application, it's useless to you in an emergency. You won't have time in an emergency to read a book. When you are cold, hungry, homeless and hurt is not the time to start back to school. Take your family camping, practice in your back yard. Get your spouse and kids involved, make a game of it. Keep in mind that you'll need to survive as a unit, and there won't be enough time for one person to do everything that has to be done in a disaster. This book is designed to provide you with many of the basic skills you'll need to care for yourself and your family when disaster strikes.

There's never a question as to whether a disaster will strike, the questions are:

- Where's it going to strike?
- When's it going to strike?
- How bad's it going to be?

SURVIVAL TIPS AND TACTICS

There are many writers who choose to present "Survival Skills" from a purist's point of view. My esteemed colleagues and peers have a sole point in their favor. It's best to know the basics of how to do something with nothing at all. That being said, I look at "Survival" in a different light, and I will preach it from the rafters with my last breath. Read this, write it down, and then commit it to memory. Survival is not a game. The primary rule for survival is to do whatever it takes to remain alive for one more day. Evaluate your circumstances before you run around wasting energy and resources. Assess what is already there for you and make use of it. Being able to rub two sticks together to start a fire is an admirable skill and one that is worthwhile to master, but it's a foolish waste of effort if you have a box of waterproof matches or a Bic lighter in your pocket. Your brain is the most powerful survival tool ever devised, use it.

There seems to be a public fascination these days with an "Apocalypse" of some sort. Television shows, movies, and novels are filled with ideas, some of which would be quite useful and others which are simply absurd. Here's a hint: the absurd ones will not merely cause you embarrassment, they'll probably result in death, serious injury, or illness...and not just for yourself, but for others you care for. Nevertheless, the final chapter of this book will contain a bulleted list of odd or unusual tips that your mind already knows about...but would never occur to you in a serious discussion of survival tips and techniques.

Should such an event actually occur, remember that strength, and therefore survival, lies in numbers. Acquiring friends is as much a necessity as knowing how to start a fire or build a shelter. The more people you can assemble, the greater your skills pool. Ten people together can make survival a much more comfortable endeavor; the group ethic and mutual encouragement are powerful survival tools, and once the basics are acquired, the mental support and reassurance will be essential to your eventual success.

So you don't believe in apocalyptic events? Perhaps a large scale natural disaster provides more of a backdrop for your worst-case scenario. Heaven knows we have enough of those. Severe weather, flooding, tornadoes, microbursts, hurricanes, drought, wildfires, the list is endless. Power outages, water contamination, the destruction of dwellings and other buildings, loss of medical care, food shortages, limited transportation options, and loss of communications are de rigueur in a natural disaster.

Are you ready, willing, and able to address those problems with only your personal knowledge, skills, and whatever resources you can marshal?

PREPAREDNESS

Are you ready to deal with disaster? Very few people have the foresight or the wherewithal to build a concrete bunker and squirrel away six months' worth of food and medical supplies, but do you have a simple survival kit stashed away in the hall closet? Do you have enough canned goods and water in the pantry to survive a few days until you can scavenge what you need for yourself and your family to thrive? Don't you think you should?

Stumbling around in soggy debris looking for a match and some dry firewood is a misery you don't need when you and your family are trying to recover from the shock that will follow a major disaster of any kind. A full belly, a warm fire, and shelter from the elements would go a long way to reassuring and calming your family. It would also assist you in remaining calm and enabling you to bring your single most important survival resource to bear on solving your problems...your mind.

Building a survival inventory doesn't require a massive investment. It can be broken down in increments over time, allowing you to put a great deal of thought and planning into what you would need or want should the worst happen...and if you watch the news every day, you'll be aware that it can happen at any moment with little or no notice. Don't be one of the victims, be one of the survivors. I will present a list of suggestions for a survival kit in a later chapter.

Several basic human needs must be met in order to simply survive until the next day: Water, fire, food, and shelter. Once those have been met, you will find you have other needs. Medical care, methods for acquiring, preserving, and storing resources. Land navigation skills, communications skills, construction skills, mechanical skills. Again, the list is endless. In the following pages, I'm going to try to familiarize you with many of these fundamental skills. Some you will have to find out for yourself, taking into consideration things like the terrain, the weather, the number of survivors around you and your geographic location. It will require a great deal of thought, and more than a little effort...but the rewards for your labors will be beyond measure. If you doubt me, look to your left and to your right, and then tell me how much your family means to you. Can you set a price tag on their lives?

A PRAGMATIC NOTE ON SCAVENGING

There is nothing more important than using your head in a survival situation, but making sure you utilize your whole family comes in a close second. They will be worried too, and the mental hardship will take its toll on them as much as on you. Keeping them occupied will be a primary task for you. Organize them. Assign them chores around the camp, like covering yesterday's waste products in your latrine.

This will have the additional benefit of cutting down the fly population around your site, and flies are notorious carriers of disease. There will be a lot less garbage than you had before the disaster, but it will have to be dealt with.

Food scraps, cans, and other debris created by your everyday life will have to be burned or buried to keep the animals from taking over your site during the night. Even young children can be assigned these tasks and it will put some much needed routine in their lives. After the disaster, getting in touch with other survivors is going to be important as well. The larger the group you can be associated with, the more protection you have, the more skills you have access to, the more hands to help with heavier projects, and, probably most importantly, the more resources you have access to. Make it a regular job after household chores every day to go out in a different direction looking for other survivors. Keep a map of the other contacts you make.

Develop a means of communicating with this group, even if it means establishing a runner route to each location if you have no radio or cell phone usage. If you have older children, split them into groups to spread the search. When you or the groups are out looking for other people, make it a habit to carry along a "harvest" bag. This bag should be as large as you can comfortably carry. You should fill this with any useful items you think you might need as you travel. Remember that storms, floods, earthquakes, hurricanes and tornadoes scatter everything they touch. You never know when you might find bottled water, canned food, matches, lighters, tools, rolls of plastic sheeting, or other useful items.

THE BASICS

MENTAL

Ordinarily the first "necessity" survival guides tell you that you need to acquire is water, but it truly is not. It's up to you to establish your priorities once you have gathered the members of your family or group together and are assured of their safety. The very first thing you absolutely must do is calm down and think about your situation. There is no room for despair or negativism in your mind. The single most important factor in any survival situation is your mental state.

A positive, can-do attitude and a clear mind is not just important to your group, it is essential to you as well. Sometimes it is necessary to alter the priorities you have learned in your reading about survival techniques. If you are in an environment where you are faced with freezing cold and rain, obviously you will need to focus on shelter and warmth before finding water. Hypothermia can kill in a matter of hours...you can last a day or two without water.

Once again, don't waste time on following a set pattern. Take stock of what is available in your immediate area and make use of what you already have at hand. Environmentalists decry the manufacture and use of plastics, but in a survival situation the non-biodegradable stuff can literally be a lifesaver. It can be used for collecting and storing water, as clothing or shelter, as bandages or splints, or any other purpose to which you can turn it...and there is virtually nowhere on earth that you can't find it in some shape or form.

After any catastrophe, there will be resources available to the people who use their heads. Lumber and plywood from destroyed structures. Metal roofing and sheathing torn from structures and blown or washed around. Cloth, leather, rubber, food, clothing...everything has a use sooner or later. Use whatever is at hand. Food, cooking utensils, dishes, brushes, brooms, any item made by man or nature; everything has a use. Playing at being Daniel

Boone is a nice fantasy, but think about it. When was the last time you were in a plane crash in the wilderness, or stranded in the desert after a car crash? The average person is far more likely to need survival skills after a catastrophic event near his own home than in a wilderness survival situation. Don't ignore the basics, but focus on more likely circumstances. *Use your head, it's your number one survival tool.* Your ability to scavenge, salvage, and improvise all come under the heading of 'mental' when it comes to survival.

WATER

Water is generally recognized as the primary need for the survivors of a catastrophic event. In some particularly harsh environments shelter may be required before water, but that matter will be addressed later under the heading of 'Shelter.'

Generally speaking, a human can survive for three days without water. More than three quarters of your body weight is comprised of fluids. You lose those fluids through heat, cold, stress, and exertion. Those fluids must be replaced for your body to function properly. At least two quarts of water are needed daily, per person, in order to maintain health.

In this day and age, bottled water seems to be available in every grocery, convenience, and variety store, as well as in vending machines. There is no need to go through the effort of boiling water, digging wells, or any of the other means of getting water if there is a nearby source of bottled water. If it's available, you can harbor your strength for the other tasks you are surely going to face. Take a walk, check your surroundings, see what's available with little effort first. Work smart, not hard.

Steer away from distilled water as much as possible, because it can leach minerals from your system over time and leave your body badly depleted. Two things are important to note here:

Drinking distilled water for a short time will not endanger your health. It would take consumption of distilled water only over a long period of time to do any real damage, so for survival purposes, don't worry about it.

Boiling water to purify it is not the same as distilling it. Distilling is a process whereby water is turned into vapor and then collected by some means and condensing it back into liquid form. It is only by this process that literally everything is removed from water, leaving it sterile.

Locating water is not as difficult as it might seem. There are four signs that lead to water: animal trails, vegetation, birds, and civilization.

Running water is the best source for drinking water. Water running over a clean, sandy bottom purifies itself every ten feet, but there is still the chance that invisible contaminants or bacteria could be present. No matter where you are, or how clear available water sources appear, if you do not have access to bottled water you must purify it before drinking it. Dysentery and cholera are not pleasant companions, and those diseases will be a severe drain on both manpower and available resources...and they can kill.

There are several methods of purifying water, but here we will confine ourselves to just a few. There are far too many other methods available to cover them all in a book of this scope.

BOILING

Raw water must be brought to a rolling boil for a period of at least one minute to purify it. Once the water has boiled long enough, it must be allowed to settle long enough for suspended particles to drift to the bottom of the container, and any floating debris can be skimmed off the top.

CHEMICAL PURIFICATION

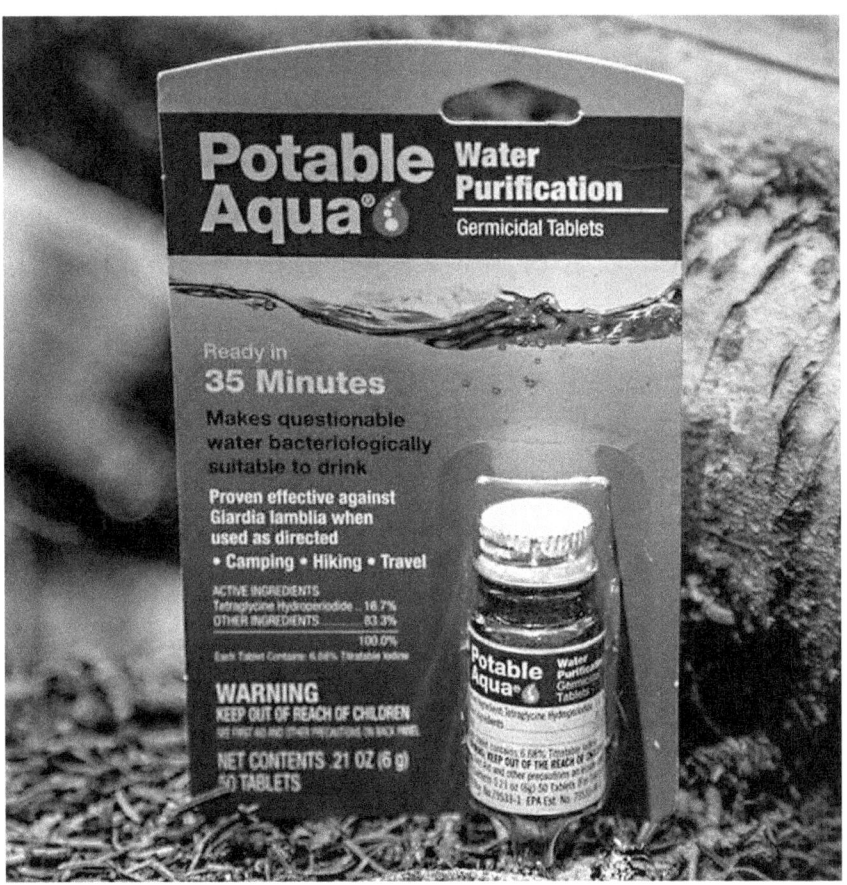

Water Treatment Tablets

Water purification tablets are commercially available both in stores and online. Instructions for their use are printed on their labels. If you don't have access to water purification tablets, add eight drops of two and one half percent iodine solution per quart of water and let it stand for 10 minutes before drinking.

FILTRATION

There are several options available for filtration of raw water. The simplest of these can be made with any two liter soft drink bottle or other container by creating three roughly equal layers, one of pea sized gravel, one of fine sand, and one of crushed charcoal.

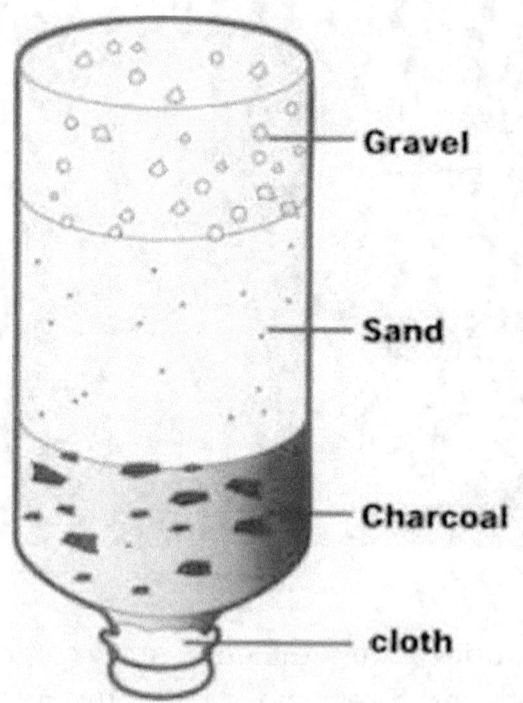

The final stage, made of cloth such as tee shirt material or linen from bedsheets, removes the last of the contaminants from the water. Always select the cleanest water available for filtration. Try to get it from flowing sources if at all possible, and try to avoid small, stagnant sources. Bacterial contaminants are the hardest to filter out, and moving water is less likely to harbor them. This same method will also work with larger containers made of glass, plastic, stone, wood, and even canvas.

FIRE

Fire building is a necessity for multiple survival needs, and even with convenient combustibles and an ignition source, fire building is a skill that simply has to be practiced in order to guarantee that you will be able harness its benefits. It looks easy enough when you see someone do it on television or in a movie, but the reality isn't quite so simple. I can't emphasize this enough. *Do not wait until your life depends on it to learn fire starting skills. Only practice will guarantee your success.*

The first step in starting any fire is collecting fuel. It should be as dry as possible, and you must collect three different types.

TINDER

Tinder is the foundation of every fire. It can be wood shavings, leaves, cotton wadding, fine straw, dried moss, tissue, paper, steel wool, thread, anything that will catch instantly and remain burning until your kindling begins to burn.

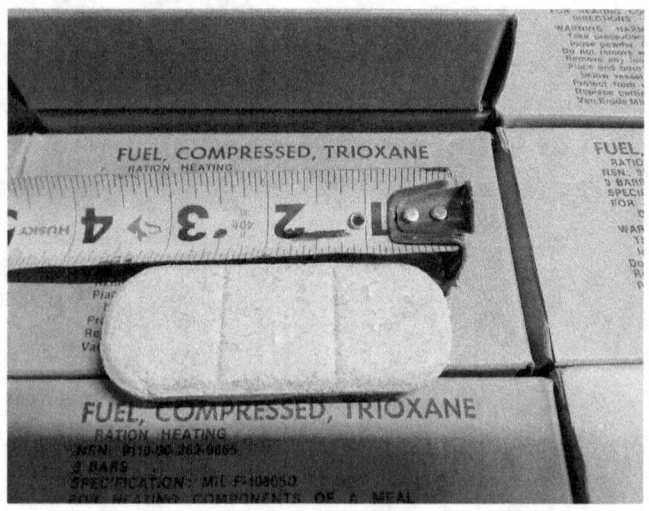

Fire Starter Trioxane Fuel Bars

One item that you can purchase commercially will have your fire started instantly, even in wet and windy situations, is a compressed trioxane fuel tablet. Massive quantities were manufactured for the military in the 1960s and are available at discount prices virtually everywhere. They ignite at the touch of a match and burn with an intense blue flame, even when wet. They are the single most useful "cheat" you could ever obtain for fire starting, followed closely by magnesium shavings, which are somewhat more difficult to find.

KINDLING

You can split wood for kindling, but it's easier to collect small twigs and branches to stack above your tinder. It needs to be thin and as dry as possible in order to catch easily, otherwise your tinder will burn up quickly and you will need to start over. Once again, use what you find around you, conserve your energy for other tasks.

FUEL

Larger limbs, branches, boards, anything that will burn can be used for fuel. A word of caution; green wood and treated lumber will smoke. Inhaling smoke from treated wood in particular can be harmful to the lungs, and in some cases, downright deadly. Extreme caution should be exercised if it is necessary to burn plastics for fuel, especially if you are in an unvented shelter.

IGNITION

Matches and disposable butane lighters are excellent ignition sources, and you should have both in your survival kit (covered later in another chapter.)

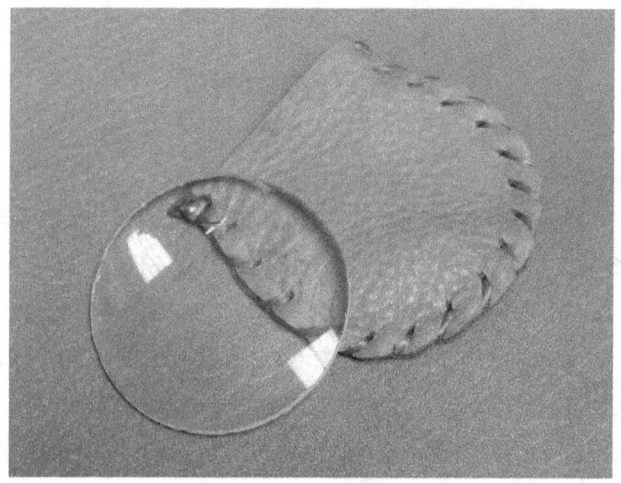

Magnifying lens

There are other methods, far more difficult for the novice, but with practice they can be mastered by nearly anyone. Please do not wait until your life depends on it to practice your fire starting skills. They should be practiced frequently so that when you need them you don't have to learn the hard way.

The simplest primitive method is the use of a magnifying lens, (providing the sun is out.) The lens should be held six to twelve inches away from the tinder and the pinpoint of light needs to be on the driest part of the tinder. Once the tinder begins to smoke, encourage it to burst into flame by blowing on it gently.

Fire Starter & Magnesium Fuel Bar

The use of flint and steel is another ignition method, a bit more difficult than using a magnifying lens. One of the most common misconceptions about the use of flint and steel is the belief that one is using the steel to scrape off pieces of the flint onto the tinder. The opposite is in fact, the truth. The flint is harder, and it chips off a tiny bit of the steel, which has to be directed towards the tinder. Agate, carnelian, jade, bloodstone, chalcedony, quartz, and chert can all be used as a substitute for flint. Hold the steel in your strong hand and strike the steel with the flint held in the other hand to direct sparks into your tinder. Hint: flakes of magnesium or iron pyrite scattered in your tinder make this a much easier option.

STRUCTURE

The fire should be laid out in whatever structure you prefer, a square, a pyramid, a tipi, any form which follows the order of tinder, kindling, and then fuel on top. If conditions are ideal, the tinder, kindling, and fuel perfectly dry, and you structure your fire in a broad pyramid or a square, the order can be reversed. It's a riskier method if you have only a single match or if you're using a more primitive method of ignition, and it is not recommended in a survival situation.

FOOD

PLANT FOOD

Plants are the most common food item on earth, and the vast majority of them are edible. Unfortunately some plants are poisonous and tasting or swallowing even a tiny portion of a poisonous plant can cause severe discomfort, severe internal illness, or even death. If you have the slightest doubt as to whether a plant is edible or not, use the universal edibility test before eating any part of it.

UNIVERSAL EDIBILITY TEST

Before bothering with the test, determine whether there are enough of them present to make testing worth your time and effort. You will need at least twenty-four hours to complete the edibility test.

- Break the plant down into its basic components, leaves, stems, roots, buds, and flowers and test only one part of the plant at a time.
- Sniff the plant element to detect strong or acidic odors, but remember that odor alone does not indicate the plant is edible.
- Refrain from eating for at least eight hours before beginning the test.

- In the hours before testing, check for contact poisoning by putting a piece of the plant on the skin inside of your elbow or wrist. Keep it in place for at least fifteen minutes contact to allow for a reaction.
- During the test, don't take anything by mouth other than purified water and the plant fragment being tested.
- Pick a small amount and prepare it in the way you intend to eat it.
- Before placing the plant portion in your mouth, take a pinch of it and touch it to the outer surface of your lip to check for burning or itching.
- Wait three minutes to see that there is on reaction on your lip. If not, put a pinch on the flat of your tongue, and hold it there for fifteen minutes.
- If you don't get a reaction, chew the pinch thoroughly and hold it in your mouth for fifteen minutes without swallowing.
- If you feel no burning, itching, numbing, stinging, or other irritation during the fifteen minutes, you can swallow the food.
- You will need to wait for eight hours, taking nothing by mouth other than purified water. If you feel any ill effects during this period, induce vomiting and drink lots of water.
- If you experience no ill effects within the eight hour period, you can go ahead and eat half a cup of the same plant part prepared in the same manner. Wait for eight more hours. If you experience no ill effects, the part of the plant as you prepared it is safe to eat.

Once again, it is imperative that you test the different parts of the plant separately. Some plants have leaves that are perfectly safe to eat and poisonous roots, and vice versa.

POISONOUS PLANTS

Do not eat unfamiliar plants that possess the following features:

- Milky sap, or a sap that turns black when exposed to air.
- Resemble mushrooms.
- Resemble onions or garlic.
- Resemble parsley, parsnip, or dill.
- Possess carrot-like leaves, roots, or tubers.

ANIMAL FOOD

Animal food has the highest food value by weight. Anything that can creep, crawl, swim, or fly is a potential source of food...but you have to catch, kill and butcher it's a viable source. There are many ways of catching fish and animals. You can catch fish by using a net across a small stream, or by making fish traps and baskets, or you can improvise fish hooks and spears like the ones in the illustration below and use them for conventional fishing, spearing and digging.

Figure 11-5. SPEARS AND FISH HOOKS

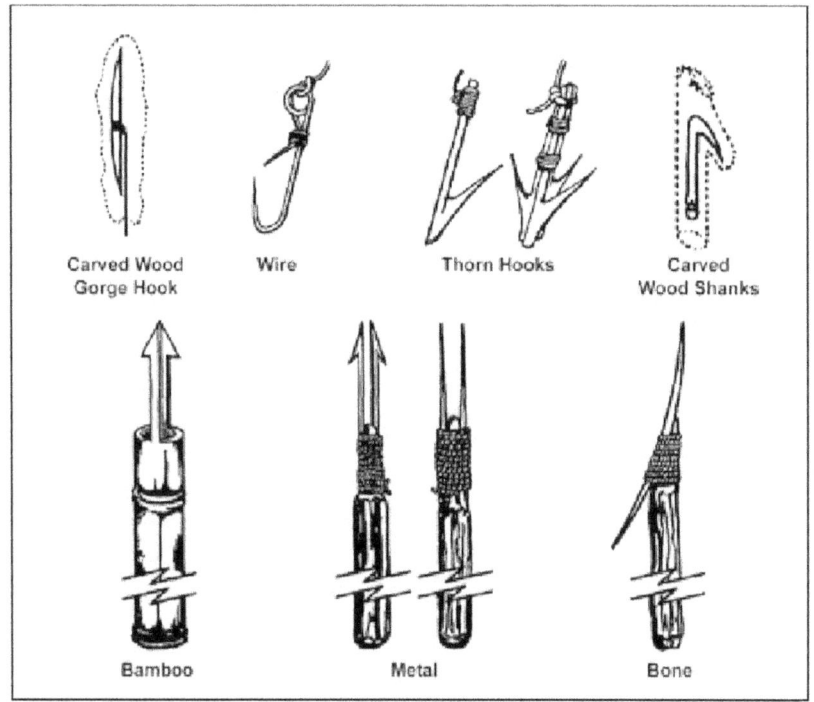

Carved Wood Gorge Hook · Wire · Thorn Hooks · Carved Wood Shanks

Bamboo · Metal · Bone

SH 21-76 UNITED STATES ARMY RANGER HANDBOOK
JULY 2006 Edition

When you begin to hunt, remember to keep it simple. In most parts of the U.S., rabbits and squirrels are far more common than people are. Rabbits can be found along nearly any roadway early in the morning, drinking the dew from grass. They usually won't even move when you walk up on them. Squirrels can be found around virtually any nut bearing hardwoods. These animals can even be found inside most cities. Become familiar with the wild game in your region, including both fish and fowls.

Take your family hunting and fishing in your leisure time...learning to shoot and clean game when you're hurting and hungry is not fun. Learn and practice your skills on family camping, hunting, and fishing trips instead of waiting to learn the hard way.

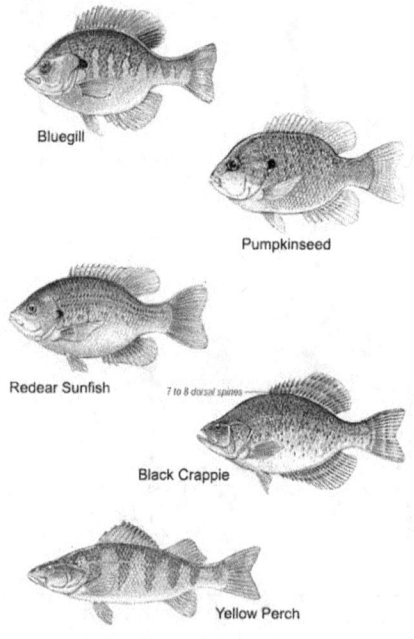

bigbluegill.com

If you've ever been fishing, you already know that the bluegill, sunfish, or bream is the most prolific fish in North American waters. If you catch one, there are generally a hundred more right beside it, they tend to cluster in schools. I learned to fish catching these small, feisty fish...and even after all this time, they are ounce for ounce one of the best fighting fish in the world (not to mention fun.) The important part is, these fish are plentiful and tasty.

TRAPS AND SNARES

If you are unarmed, trapping or snaring game is your only option. Using multiple well-placed traps, you are likely to have a chance to catch much more game than you would be likely to find and shoot.

To be successful with any kind of trap or snare, you have to know what kind of animal you want to catch, know how to build a proper trap for that type of animal, and then manage to avoid alarming the critter with signs or smells of your presence.

TRAPS

There's no catchall trap you can set out for all animals. You have to know what animals live in your area and set your traps specifically for them. If you aren't familiar with the local fauna, look for the following:

- Runs or trails.
- Tracks.
- Droppings.
- Gnawed or rubbed vegetation.
- Nesting or roosting sites.

- Feeding and watering areas.

POSITIONING

Place your traps and snares where you find proof that the critters come by. When you locate animal sign, you have to decide whether you have found a "run" or a "trail."

A trail will show signs of use by several types of animals and it will be rather noticeable. A run is usually smaller and less noticeable, and it will only contain signs of one type of animal. You can build a perfect snare, but it won't catch anything if just set it out randomly in the woods. Animals, like people, are creatures of habit, and they tend to repeat behavior that has proven successful. They follow the same trails to bedding areas, water sources, and feeding areas until those trails prove dangerous to them. You have to place snares and traps around these areas to catch them.

Refrain from creating any kind of disruption that will alarm the animal and make it to circumvent the trap. If you have to dig, make sure you take all fresh dirt away from the area around the trap or snare. Most critters will intuitively stay away from a pitfall-type trap.

Build your device away from the place you want to set it, and carry it in to set it up. That way you won't disturb the local vegetation and spook your prey. Don't use freshly cut, live vegetation to construct a trap or snare. Freshly cut foliage will "bleed" sap that has a smell that the animal will be able to detect, and it will set off its flight response.

You must also disguise or simply remove any scent of your presence on and around the trap you've set. Birds don't have a developed sense of smell, nearly all other animals are more dependent on scent than on sight. The slightest hint of human scent on a trap will spook your prey and, and it probably will not return to the area for a long time, if ever. Taking the scent off your device is difficult, but camouflaging your odor is fairly easily done. You can smear the fluids from the gall and urine bladders of earlier kills on the trap, but don't use human urine. Mud, especially from an area with lots of decaying vegetation, works as well. Coat your hands before handling your trap and spread it on the trap when you set it.

Animals recognize the odor of burned vegetation and smoke, but they're only alarmed when a fire is actually burning. Smoking the trap parts is an effective method of concealing your scent.

Another alternative is to build the trap and then let it weather for a few days before setting it. Make sure to coat your hands with a masking scent before you place the trap, and make sure that you camouflage it well, making it look as much like its surroundings as possible to prevent from being sensed by your prey.

CANALIZATION

When you are setting a trap or snare along a run or a trail, build a channel, a funnel-shaped impediment reaching from the edges of the trail toward the trap, with the narrowest portion closest to the trap itself. The canalization should be unobtrusive enough that the animal isn't alerted in any way. As it approaches the trap, it should not be able to change direction and avoid the trap. Most animals won't back up, they prefer to face their direction of travel. Canalization should never be an impenetrable barrier, it only needs to guide your prey. Animals, much like people and water, tend to take the path of least resistance. Simple inconvenience is usually enough to keep him on the path to your trap. In order for the canalization to be truly effective, it should narrow the path down to a little wider than the animal itself for at least the length of its body before it reaches the trap.

SNARES

A snare is nothing more than a sliding that can tighten and strangle or hold any creature caught in it. You can use heavy twine, bootlaces, thin wire, cordage made by weaving strips of the bark of small hardwood saplings together, or hide strips from previously caught animals to build snares.

Treadle snare

Figure 11-6. TREADLE SNARE

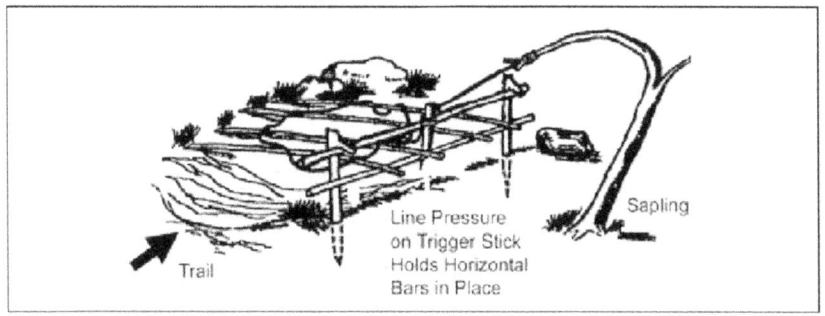

SH 21-76 UNITED STATES ARMY RANGER HANDBOOK
JULY 2006 Edition

Treadle snares are very useful on small game on a trail, but they are a fairly difficult snare to construct. Excavate a shallow hole in the trail, then place the sticks with the forked ends pointing downwards as in the illustration below, into the ground on either side of the hole on the sides of the trail. Pick two relatively straight sticks that reach between the two forks and place one of them so the forks engage its ends. The other straight stick goes below the first. Put several sticks over the hole in the trail by placing one end over the lower stick and the other on the ground opposite the hole. Cover the hole with enough sticks so that the animal is forced to step on at least one of them to trigger the snare.

Tie one end of a piece of light cordage to a bent sapling or to a weight slightly heavier than your prey and suspend it over a tree limb. Bend the sapling or raise the suspended weight to determine where you will tie a two inch long loop to hold your trigger. Make a noose on the other end of the cordage.

Spread the noose over the top of the sticks lying over the hole. Place the trigger stick against the horizontal sticks and route the line behind the sticks so that tension from the sapling or weight will hold it in place. Adjust the bottom horizontal stick so that the slightest pressure will release the trigger. As the critter puts its weight on one of the sticks across the hole, the bottom horizontal stick will move down, springing the trigger and permitting the noose to tighten around the animal. This trap more than any other requires the canalization technique.

Drag noose snare

Figure 11-7. DRAG NOOSE SNARE

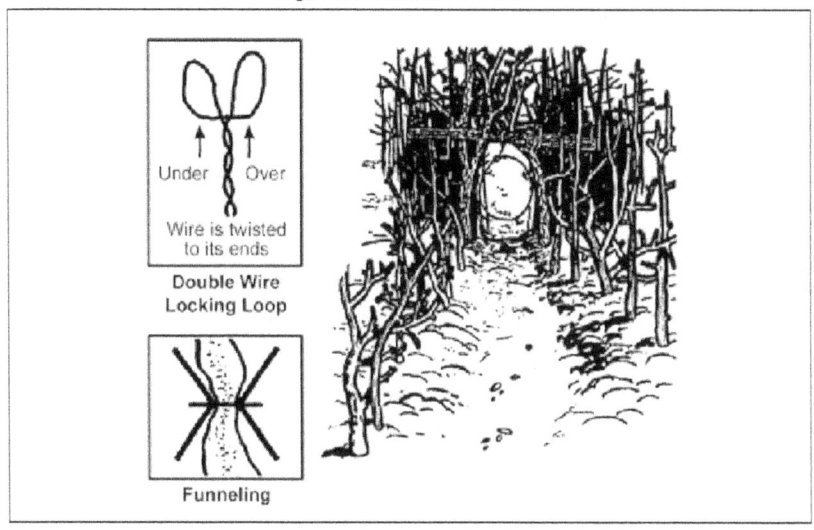

SH 21-76 UNITED STATES ARMY RANGER HANDBOOK
JULY 2006 Edition

The drag noose snare is one of the easiest snares to make and fastest to set. It's really great for catching rabbits.

Make a loop in your cordage using a bowline. Run the other end of the string (or wire) through the loop to form a noose that is big enough for the prey's head but too small for its body; tie the string or wire to a strong branch. The branch should be big enough to reach across the trail and rest on the bush or the support (two short forked sticks) you have chosen. When your prey is snared, it will free the drag stick, tugging it until it becomes entrapped in the brush. As the prey struggles to escape, the noose tightens, strangling or retaining the animal.

CLEANING AND PRESERVING ANIMAL FOODS

Once you have acquired your fish or game, you've got to clean it, butcher it, cook it, and store it. If you make a mistake doing any of this, all of your efforts will have been for nothing.

You have to know how to determine whether fish are free of bacterial decay that makes the fish dangerous to eat. Although cooking might be able to obliterate the toxins from rotting, don't eat fish that seem spoiled.

FISH

SIGNS OF SPOILAGE

• Strange odor.

• Irregular color. (Gills must be pink or red. Scales ought to be a pronounced and unfaded shade of gray).

• Depression remains after pressing your thumb against the flesh.

• Slimy body.

• Sharp or peppery taste.

Consuming bad fish can cause diarrhea, nausea, cramps, vomiting, itching, paralysis, or a metallic taste in your mouth. Any of these symptoms can occur suddenly one to six hours later. If you have access to sea water, drink it immediately at the onset of the symptoms and force yourself to regurgitate. If you don't have salt water, use a feather or your finger to induce vomiting.

Fish spoil quickly, particularly on a hot days, so they must be prepared for eating as quickly as possible after they've been caught. Remove the gills and the large blood vessels next to the backbone. You don't have to remove the head if you intend to spit the fish and roast it over a fire. Any fish more than four inches long must be gutted after making an incision from anus to gills along the abdomen and then scraping out the intestines. Once the fish is gutted, you can either scale or skin the fish.

COOKING

A fish can be spitted and roasted, or pan fried, but it has far more nutritional value if it is boiled with the skin still on it. The fats and oil are beneath the skin, and if you boil the fish, the remaining liquid makes a nutritious broth. Any of the methods you use for cooking can be used for cooking fish...and you can tell it is done when the meat flakes off.

You can preserve fish by drying them in the sun, either hanging them from branches or spreading them on hot rocks. When the fish is dried, splash it with sea water, if available, or salt the outside. You should only keep fish or other seafood if it is well dried or salted.

SNAKES

All snakes are edible. Follow these steps to prepare snakes for eating:

- Grab the snake firmly behind its head and sever it with a sharp blade.
- Slit the belly and remove the guts. (You may use the guts to bait traps or snares.)
- Remove the skin. (The skin is useful in improvising, belts, straps, or other, similar items).

Figure 11-11. CLEANING A SNAKE

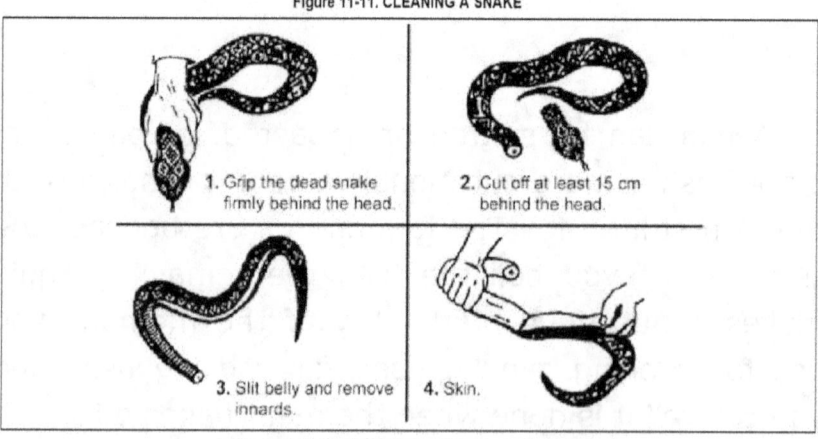

1. Grip the dead snake firmly behind the head.

2. Cut off at least 15 cm behind the head.

3. Slit belly and remove innards.

4. Skin.

SH 21-76 UNITED STATES ARMY RANGER HANDBOOK
JULY 2006 Edition

CAUTION: Be very careful catching snakes. Some snakes are venomous to be fatal. Even after the head is severed, reflex action can cause it to bite and inject its venom into you. The best time to catch a snakes is early in the morning or late in the evening when temperatures are lower and reptiles tend to move slower. Use a long forked stick to pin its head to the ground and place your index finger on the top rear of its head with your thumb and middle finger on either side of the head behind its jaws. If you keep your index finger on top of the snake's head you will prevent it from turning within its skin and biting you.

CLEANING FOWL

The first step after acquiring a fowl of any kind is to pluck its feathers. If plucking is not practical, you can skin it. Bear in mind that a fowl cooked with the skin on holds greater food value. Waterfowl are easier to pluck when they are dry, but other birds are easier to pluck after you scald them. After plucking the feathers, sever its neck close to the body. Slice open the abdominal cavity and remove the guts. The neck, liver, and heart should be retained for use in stews or soups, but the rest can be used as bait for fishing, snares, and traps. Clean the abdominal cavity with fresh, pure water. Boil fowl or spitting it over a fire are the recommended methods of preparation. If you should happen upon a scavenger bird such as a vulture or a buzzard, you have to boil it for at least twenty minutes to eliminate any parasites.

Bird feathers can be used for insulation of shoes, clothing, or bedding. You can also use them to make fishing lures.

CLEANING MEDIUM-SIZED MAMMALS

Figure 11-12. SKINNING AND BUTCHERING LARGE GAME

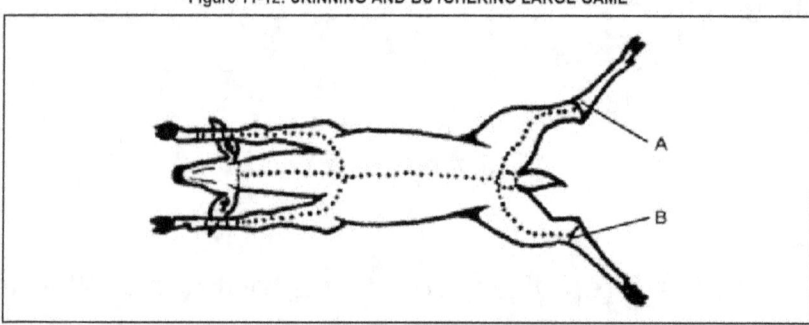

Figure 11-13. SKINNING SMALL GAME

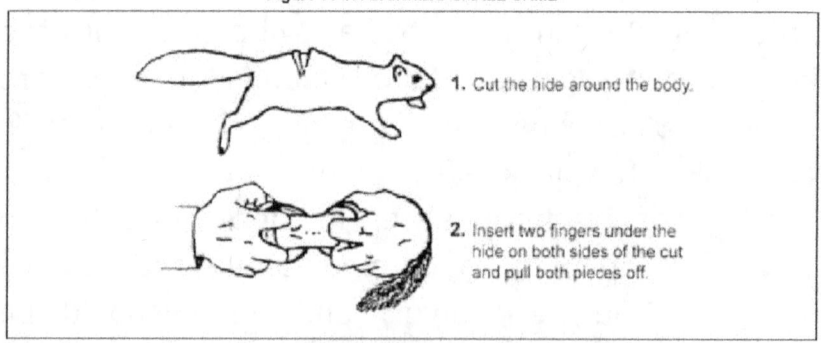

1. Cut the hide around the body.

2. Insert two fingers under the hide on both sides of the cut and pull both pieces off.

SH 21-76 UNITED STATES ARMY RANGER HANDBOOK
JULY 2006 Edition

Any game you manage to trap or snare will usually still be alive when you find it, and that means it's dangerous. Approach a trapped animal cautiously, and use whatever you have for a weapon to kill it, keeping a safe distance from it. After it's dead, bleed it by cutting its throat as soon as possible. If you have to drag the carcass, do it before you skin it so that the carcass is protected from dirt and debris that would contaminate it. Better yet, build a travois from two poles and keep it off the ground.

Try to clean your prey near a stream or other fresh running water so that you can wash and cool the carcass and the edible parts. Fleas and parasites will leave a cooled body so if your situation permits, wait until it cools before cleaning and dressing the carcass.

CLEANING SMALL GAME

Place carcass belly up, preferably on a slope. Use whatever is at hand to prop it up, rocks, brush, or logs. Sever and remove genitals or the udder, and the take out the musk glands so the meat won't get tainted. Make an incision in the hide from the tail to the throat, taking care to keep the cut shallow so that you don't penetrate the stomach. Slip your blade beneath the skin, again being careful not to penetrate the body cavity. Pull the hide back several inches on each side to keep from getting hair in the meat. Break open the chest cavity by cracking the sternum or cutting to either side of the sternum where the ribs converge.

Sever the windpipe and gullet as near to the base of the skull as you can. After the forward end of the intestinal tract is free, work your way down the carcass, lifting out the internal organs and the intestines. Make cuts only when you have to in order to free them. Remove the bladder carefully and quickly get it away from the carcass so you do not pierce the bladder and taint the meat. Pinch the urethra tightly and sever it past the point where you are pinching. Take out the bladder. Cut a circle around the anus from the outside and tug the anus inside the body cavity and out of the carcass. Elevate or rotate the carcass so that the blood will drain.

Note: Try to save as much of the blood as you can because it's a vital source of food and salt. Boil the blood to eliminate any parasites before using it as a food source.

Peel off the hide, and making cuts along the inside of the legs to a point just above the hoofs or paws. Use your blade in a slicing motion to cut the membrane between the skin and meat when you're removing the hide.

Every part of an animal can be used. Heart, liver, and kidneys can be eaten. Slice open the heart to remove any blood from its chambers. Open the kidneys and flush them with fresh water; if enough water is available, soak them. In every animals except the ones of the deer family, the gall bladder is fastened to the liver. Sometimes, the sac looks a little like a blister on the liver. Take out the sac by holding the upper portion of it and slicing the liver around and behind the sac. If the gall bladder is punctured, flush the bladder immediately so the meat doesn't become tainted. Throw the gall away. Any clean blood splattered on the meat will glaze over and help keep the meat preserved for a little while, but if the carcass is not properly bled, blood will pool in the lowest parts and will cause the meat to spoil in short order. Remove any meat that has become contaminated.

Below forty degrees Fahrenheit, meat can be left hanging for several days with no danger of going bad. If you cannot keep the flies off the carcass and maggots get on the meat, scrape off there the maggots and slice off the tainted meat. What's left will be edible. If food is *really* scarce, maggots are an excellent source of protein and can be eaten as well. Disgusting as they are, they are useful creatures. They can be used in the treatment of gangrenous wounds because they only eat dead flesh.

THE REST OF THE ANIMAL

Blood is a source of salts and other nutrients, and makes a good base for soups. The intestines, once thoroughly cleaned, can be used for storing or smoking food, or to make lashings for weapons, snares, and construction or for general use. The tendons and ligaments can also be used for lashings. If you don't dry them thoroughly they will rot.

The heads of most animals contain a great deal of meat, and it's fairly easy to get it. Skin the head and save the skin for leather. Cleanse the mouth thoroughly and remove the tongue. The outer skin can be removed from the tongue after cooking. Odd as it may seem, tongue can be found in most grocery outlets in the U.S. You can cut or scrape the meat from the head, or you can roast the head over an open fire before collecting the meat. The eyes are edible. They can be cooked and eaten, but be careful to throw away the retinas, which are very much like plastic and can't be digested. Many people consider brains to be a delicacy, but they are also useful in tanning hides. Bone marrow is a nutrient rich food source. Crack the bones and scrape the marrow out, and then use the bones for any purpose you can imagine...buttons, weapons, utensils, the list is only limited by your imagination.

PRESERVATION

If at all possible, you should preserve extra meat for use at a later time. After a major catastrophe, there is no certainty as to when supplies will become available again. If the ambient air temperature is low enough, you can freeze the meat. In warmer climates, you will have to drying or smoke the meat or fish to preserve it. One night of heavy smoking will keep meat safe to eat for about a week. After two nights of heavy smoking the meat will stay edible for two to four weeks.

Figure 11-14. SMOKING MEAT

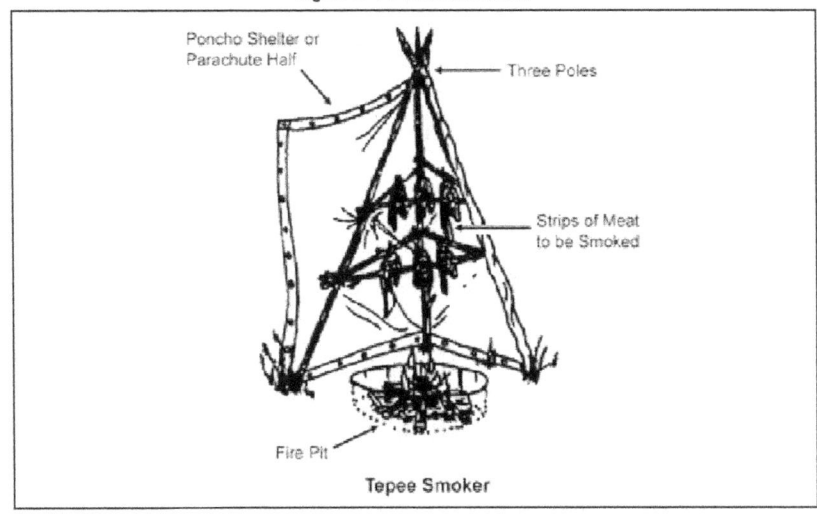

Poncho Shelter or Parachute Half

Three Poles

Strips of Meat to be Smoked

Fire Pit

Tepee Smoker

SH 21-76 UNITED STATES ARMY RANGER HANDBOOK
JULY 2006 Edition

To prepare meat for curing, it needs to be cut with the grain in quarter inch strips. You can air dry the meat, by hanging it in the wind and hot sun, out of reach of scavengers. It should be covered in order to keep the flies off it.

You will need an enclosed space, like a small cave, a tent, a teepee, or a pit, to cure the meat in. You will also need green wood, but you can't use conifers such as pines, firs, spruces, or cedars, because the resinous smoke from these types of trees impart a bitter, acidic flavor to the meat.

Ensure that when using an enclosed area the top is vented and place the fire in the center. The wood must burn down to coals, and then green wood should be laid on the burning coals. The meat strips should be laid on a grate or suspended from the top of the enclosure about two feet above the fire.

If you prefer to use the pit method, you will need to dig a hole about three feet deep and a foot and a half in diameter. The fire should be laid in the bottom of the hole, and after it's burning well, chipped green wood or small branches of green wood should be added to create the smoke. A wooden grate will need to be suspended about one and a half feet over the fire and the meat will need to be laid atop that. Once everything is in readiness, the pit will have to be laid over with poles, and then covered with boughs, leaves, or some other material.

SHELTER

There are any number of shelters types. At the risk of being redundant, do not waste time building a shelter if any building, remnant of a building, or a ready-made structure such as a cave is available. The shelters described here are temporary in nature and should not be considered for long term use. If you have the storage space available, you might consider reviewing Army surplus sites for tentage. The GP Small, GP Medium, and GP Large tents are sturdy, vented for gas heaters, and have liners to guard against extremes of heat and cold, and they are made of stout canvas that will last almost indefinitely with care.

PONCHO LEAN-TO

Figure 11-15. PONCHO LEAN-TO

SH 21-76 UNITED STATES ARMY RANGER HANDBOOK
JULY 2006 Edition

The Poncho Lean-to takes very little in terms of time and resources to build. You need a poncho, a sheet of plastic film, or any other water resistant material, six to ten feet of rope, three stakes about six inches long that can be made of anything handy, and two poles, or trees seven to nine feet apart.

You need to check the wind direction before you select the trees or decide where to locate the poles. Ensure that when your shelter is built it is oriented so that the front will be facing away from the prevailing winds.

- Tie the hood of the poncho off by pulling the drawstring tight, rolling the hood lengthwise, and folding it into thirds. Then use the end of the draw cord to tie it off. If you are using something other than a poncho, place a small stone on the material where you need another attachment point, fold the material around it and tie it off.

- Divide the rope in half.
- On a long side of the poncho, tie one of the rope halves to the corner grommet, and the other corner grommet on the other end.
- Attach a four inch drip stick to each rope one to three-quarters of an inch away from the grommets. The drip sticks will keep water from running down the lines into the inside of the lean-to. Attach strings roughly four inches long to each of the grommets along the top edge of the poncho permit water to run to and down the line without dripping inside the shelter.
- Tie the ropes roughly waist high on the poles or trees. Using a round turn and two half hitches with quick-release knot to secure them.
- Spread the poncho or other material and use stakes to secure it to the ground.
- If you anticipate bad weather or intend to use the lean-to for a longer period of time, construct a center support by stretching a line between two uprights in line with the center of the poncho.
- Tie another line to the poncho hood or the tie-off you made earlier, lifting the center of the poncho or other material. Tie the line to the rope spanning the two uprights.

Another alternative is to cut a stick tall enough to raise the roof and use it as an upright inside the shelter, but remember that this alternative will leave you less freedom of movement under the shelter.

If you require more protection from the elements, stack boughs, branches, brush, some of your equipment at the open ends of the shelter.

Use leaves, pine needles, straw, or moss as an insulating material on the ground inside your shelter both for comfort and as insulation to retain heat.

Note: When you're at rest, you can lose as much as 80 percent of your body heat to the ground.

PRIMITIVE LEAN-TO

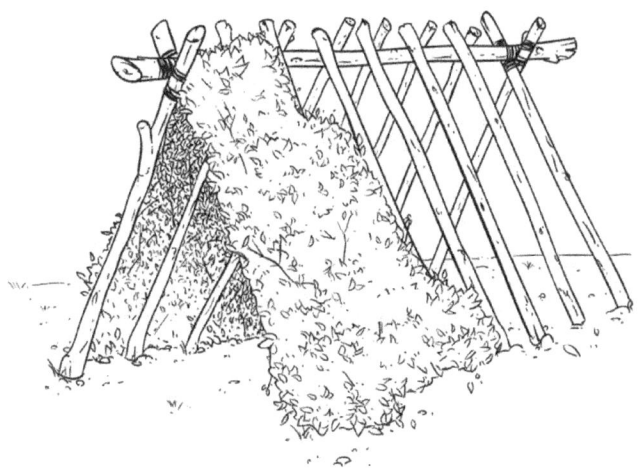

http://gearpatrol.com/2014/11/11/wilderness-guide-to-natural-shelters/

In a wooded area there should be enough raw materials to build a lean-to using nothing more than a knife. You'll need more time to build it than you did for the Poncho Lean-To, but it should protect you from the weather. You'll require two trees, or two uprights, placed about 6 feet apart, and one pole roughly seven feet long. It will take five to eight more poles roughly ten feet long to use as beams, and some type of cordage for securing the horizontal pole to the trees or other poles. It's a primitive shelter, and the illustration is self-explanatory. Just remember to utilize whatever materials are easiest to acquire.

FIRST AID

LIFESAVING STEPS

On general principles, it is a good idea for you and as many of your family members to take an approved First Aid course, as well as investing in a fairly sophisticated First Aid Kit. Experts estimate that in the course of a catastrophe, more lives are lost in the aftermath of the event than are lost in the initial event itself. This is primarily due to the lack of available medical resources. This is an additional reason to expand your group. Shock is a life-threatening condition that requires medical care beyond the scope of Basic First Aid training. If at all possible, evacuate the individual to the nearest medical facility.

Regardless of the injury being treated, always follow these steps:

- *Check to see that the airway is open and restore breathing;*
- *Stop the bleeding and safeguard the wound;*

- *Check for shock and treat if necessary. Continue to monitor for shock.*

PRIMARY SURVEY

Use the ABC's listed below to assist you in remembering how to identify and manage life-threatening injuries, airway problems, breathing difficulties, or uncontrolled bleeding.

AIRWAY MANAGEMENT

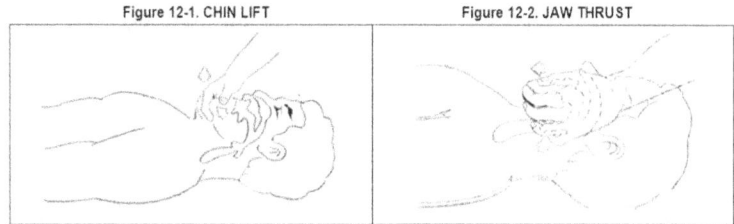

Figure 12-1. CHIN LIFT   Figure 12-2. JAW THRUST

SH 21-76 UNITED STATES ARMY RANGER HANDBOOK
JULY 2006 Edition

- Most of the time, the airway is blocked at the base of the tongue. When the airway is obstructed, open it using the chin lift or jaw thrust.

- Remove debris from the airway: (teeth, blood clots, bone) from the mouth; use suction if you have it; and use some type of device (hollow tubes, drinking straws, disposable pen bodies) to allow the patient to continue to breathe through their nose.

BREATHING

If your patient is having difficulty breathing:

- Expose the chest and check for open chest injuries;
- Use a bandage or dressing that closes the wound and keeps it from the air (an occlusive dressing) over the open entry and exit wounds. If a medical grade bandage or dressing is not in your survival kit, clean plastic wrap, the soft plastic that comes from the dry cleaners to protect your clothing, or any other non-permeable material will suffice. Make sure to secure the dressing in such a manner as too guarantee that air will not pass under the dressing. Roll your patient onto his injured side, or into a position where he can breathe most comfortably.

BLEEDING

Identify and control bleeding as quickly as possible.

- Cover the bleeding wound with a standard or pressure dressing if you have one. If one is not available, use the softest, cleanest gauze or cloth available.

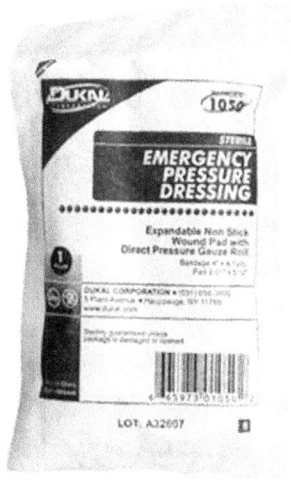

Emergency Pressure Dressing

- If the bleeding doesn't stop immediately, apply a tourniquet between the wound and the heart. Expedient tourniquets can be made with lengths of rope, neckties, belts...anything you can wrap around the appendage and tighten. A sturdy stick can be inserted and then twisted to tighten the tourniquet, but make sure you don't get it too tight; you are highly restricting the blood flow, not shutting it off completely.

- Monitor the dressings often to ensure that the bleeding is under control.

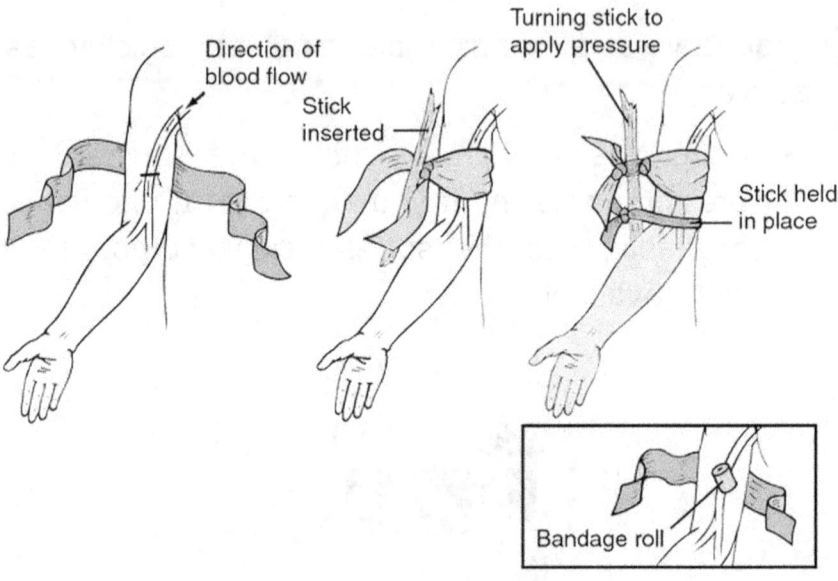

http://medical-dictionary.thefreedictionary.com/tourniquet

SHOCK

Shock causes oxygen deprivation to the tissues. It may or may not cause bleeding. The symptoms of shock can include increased pulse rate, increased respiration rate, and a lowered level of consciousness. To treat for shock:

- Open the airway
- Restore breathing
- Control bleeding
- Continue to monitor the patient's condition.

Ideally, you should start an IV of saline solution, but that is going to be beyond the skill level of most of you unless you have received some rather intensive First Aid training.

EXTREMITY INJURIES

Locate, identify and control the bleeding. If you think your patient has a fracture, splint it without moving him, and don't try to straighten or set it.

ABDOMINAL INJURIES

Locate, identify and control the bleeding. Treat the patient for shock.

- If internal organs are uncovered, place a dry, sterile dressing over it. Do not attempt to place his organs back inside the wound...don't even touch them.

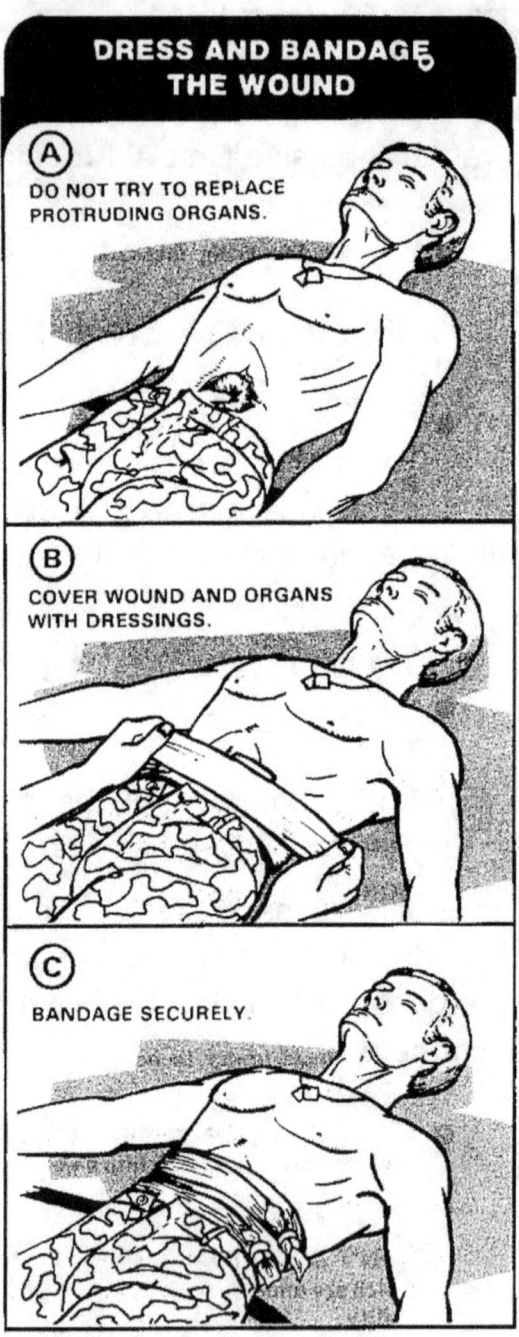

DRESS AND BANDAGE THE WOUND

A DO NOT TRY TO REPLACE PROTRUDING ORGANS.

B COVER WOUND AND ORGANS WITH DRESSINGS.

C BANDAGE SECURELY.

U.S. Army Field Manual FM 21-75
Combat Skills of the Soldier

- Place your patient in a comfortable position, and flex his knees to relax his abdominal muscles.
- Do not try to give anything to the patient by mouth.

Even if you have sophisticated First Aid Training, you must make an effort to get this patient to some sort of medical facility. The likelihood of infection is enormous, and if that doesn't kill your patient, the shock is likely to.

BURNS

Get the patient away from whatever has burned him. Once you're all safely away from the burn source:

- Remove any clothing or jewelry from the burned area
- Place dry, sterile dressings or a reasonable substitute over it, ensuring that injured fingers and toes have dressings between them before covering the burn.
- Any patient with burns of the face, neck, hands, genitalia, or over 20 percent of his body surface has a life threatening injury that

absolutely requires sophisticated medical attention.

WEATHER INJURIES.

HEAT CRAMPS

Patient has muscle cramps in arms, legs, stomach, or all of the above. Other symptoms of heat cramps are damp skin and extreme thirst.

- Move your patient to a shaded area and loosen his clothing.
- Allow your patient to drink one quart of cool water slowly per hour.
- Monitor the patient and continue rehydration at the recommended rate.

HEAT EXHAUSTION

Symptoms include loss of appetite, headache, excess sweating, weakness, faintness, dizziness, nausea, muscle cramps, and moist, pale, and clammy skin.

- Move the patient to a cool, shady area and loosen his clothing.
- Drip water over the patient, and fan him encourage evaporation of the water, which will cool him.
- Have the patient consume a minimum of one quart of water to replenish his fluids.
- Elevate the patient's legs.

As with other serious conditions, Heat Exhaustion is a medical emergency and the patient should be transported to a medical facility as soon as possible. Uncontrolled, it can advance to Heatstroke in a matter of minutes.

HEATSTROKE (SUNSTROKE)

Symptoms: The patient will stop sweating and his skin will be hot and dry. Other symptoms include headache, dizziness, nausea, vomiting, rapid pulse and respiration, seizures, and disorientation. The patient could suddenly collapse and become unconscious. This is a medical emergency and your patient needs a physician.

COLD INJURIES

CHILBLAIN

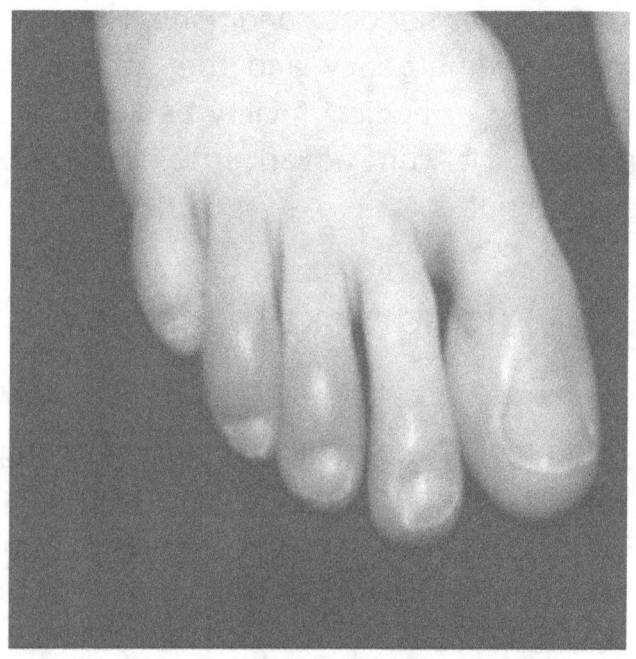

http://www.skincareihub.com/chilblains

Chilblain symptoms are red, swollen, hot, tender, and itching skin. Infected skin lesions that are ulcerated and bleeding can occur if exposure to cold continues.

- The best emergency treatment is shared body heat directly on the affected area.

- Under no circumstances should the affected areas be rubbed or massaged.
- Advanced medical treatment should be sought.

IMMERSION FOOT (TRENCH FOOT)

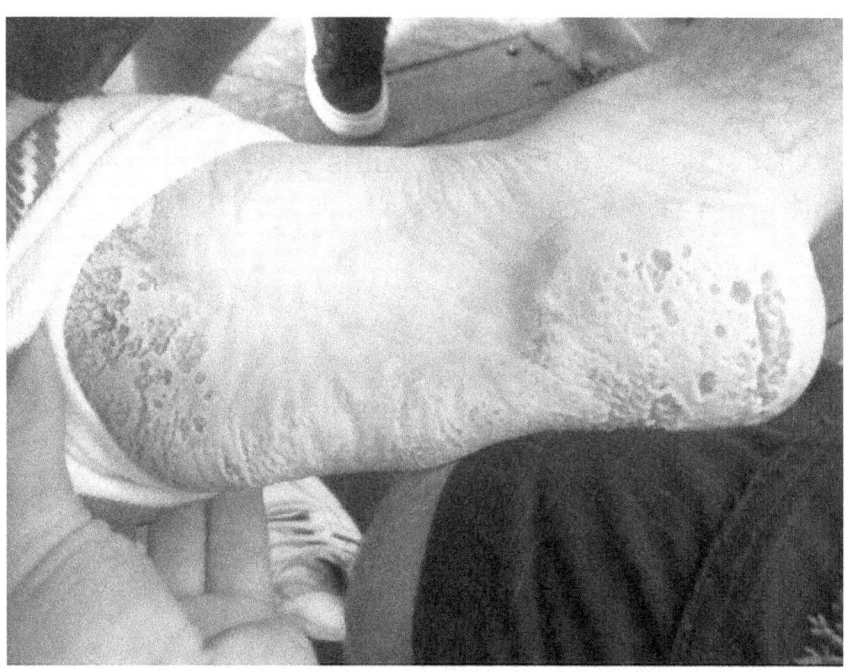

http://www.guardianfirstaid.co.uk/

The distressed areas become cold, numb, and no longer feel painful. As the areas warm up, they may feel hot, and the patient will feel burning and shooting pains. If Immersion Foot has reached the advanced stage, the patient's skin will appear pale and have a bluish cast. His pulse rate will slow down, and blistering, swelling, heat hemorrhages, and gangrene could follow.

- Warm the areas gradually by exposing them to warm air.
- Under no circumstances should you apply water or massage the skin of the affected area.
- Affected areas should be protected to keep them from being bumped or bruised.
- Pat the affected areas dry gently with a soft cloth and don't let the patient walk.

This is yet another circumstance that requires care from a medical professional.

FROSTBITE

www.haikudeck.com

SUPERFICIAL

Much like sunburn, the skin reddens. Blisters will follow in twenty-four to thirty six hours, and the skin will peel or slough off.

- Keep the patient warm, use body heat to gently warm affected areas.
- Loosen constrictive clothing, insulate the patient and encourage him to move around to increase circulation and generate body heat.

DEEP

Superficial frostbite will occur first, which is why treatment is critical. Skin loses sensation and becomes pale, yellowish, waxy, and "wooden" to the touch. Blisters will begin to form in twelve to thirty-six hours. Skin will swell and crack, and the tissue turns black. Shield the affected area from further injury, and seek immediate medical assistance. The images of deep frostbite are unnecessarily gruesome. I don't need to illustrate this injury, you will recognize it.

DEHYDRATION (COMPARABLE TO HEAT EXHAUSTION)

Most people are surprised to find that dehydration can be a cold weather injury, but the sad truth is that it is one of the most common of all cold weather injuries. Cold, dry air leaches moisture from the soft tissues of your mouth and your nose. Each time you breathe you experience moisture loss. Additionally, most people tend to dress too warmly for cold weather, causing them to perspire. Remember that the best methods for keeping warm in the cold are wearing loose clothing and keeping active. If you aren't a little cold when you're sitting or standing still, you are dressed too warmly.

- Keep the patient warm. Bulky parkas or loose blankets will provide dead air space around the patient. Dead air space is the single most effective factor in insulating the patient from the cold.
- Loosen any tight clothing articles.
- Replace lost fluids, rest, and seek additional medical treatment.

HYPOTHERMIA

A hypothermia victim will be cold and will shiver uncontrollably. If his core temperature drops below ninety-five degrees Fahrenheit, he could lose consciousness. His actions will become uncoordinated, and shock and coma may result if his body temperature continues to drop.

- Don't delay, warm the patient's body up evenly with an external heat source.
- Shelter the patient and keep him dry.
- If the patient is conscious, you can give him small quantities of warm liquids.
- CPR may become necessary if the patient stops breathing. (Covered in another chapter.)
- Seek immediate medical help.

ENVIRONMENTAL INJURIES

SNAKE BITE

- Move the patient away from the snake.
- Take all jewelry or other restrictive items off the affected extremity.
- Keep the patient quiet and reassure him.
- Place a constricting band one to two inches above the bite between the bite and the heart, taking care to leave enough room that you can insert a finger between the band and the skin.

     A. ARM OR LEG BITE - Place a band above and beneath the fang marks.

     B. HAND OR FOOT BITE - Place a band above the wrist or ankle.

- Position the patient so that his heart is above the level of the bite and immobilize him.
- If medical assistance is available, kill the snake without endangering yourself or harming the

head and send it along with the patient to the medical facility.
- Anti-venin should only be administered by a qualified individual.

SPIDER BITE

(BROWN RECLUSE OR BLACK WIDOW)

- Calm the patient.
- Clean the bite area thoroughly.
- Hold ice or a freeze pack from your First Aid kit against the bite area.
- Get medical treatment as soon as possible.

TARANTULA BITE, SCORPION STING, ANT BITE

- Clean the bite area thoroughly.
- Hold ice or a freeze pack from your First Aid kit against the bite area.
- Make a paste of baking soda or meat tenderizer and apply it to the bite site, or use calamine lotion. This will help to relieve the pain and itching.

- If the affected area is on a sensitive area like the face, neck (possible airway blockage), or genitals, if the patient's reaction is severe, or if the patient was stung by a Southwestern scorpion (particularly lethal), keep the patient as calm as possible, and inject the patient with an epinephrine auto-injector (EAI, or Epi pen) and immediately transport to a medical facility.

WASP OR BEE STING

After you've been stung, there is no remedy for bee venom and there's no way to suck the venom out of your skin. All you can do is find a way to alleviate the symptoms. When a bee stings, it leaves behind its stinger and its venom sac.

- Remove the stinger by scraping it off with a knife or finger nail, taking care not to squeeze the venom sac and inject more venom into the skin.
- Clean the affected area.
- Hold ice or a freeze pack from your First Aid kit against the sting area. I have often found a paste made of tobacco and saliva reduces the pain of the sting.

HUMAN AND OTHER ANIMAL BITES

- Clean the bite area thoroughly with soap or detergent and water.
- Rinse the area thoroughly.
- Place a sterile dressing over the wound.
- The affected appendage should be immobilized to limit blood circulation.
- Human bites are worse than animal bites, though the trauma may be less severe. Any bite is serious and requires treatment by qualified medical personnel.
- In the event of an animal bite, you should kill the animal without imperiling risking being bitten yourself or harming its head so that you can the head along with the patient to a medical facility.
- In the event of a human bites, try to isolate and preserve some saliva from the bitten area and send that in a sealed and marked container along with the patient to a medical facility.

POISONOUS PLANTS

Poison Ivy, Oak, Sumac

- Clean the affected area thoroughly with soap or detergent and water and then wash the patient's clothing.
- Coat the surface of the affected area lightly with anti-itch lotion, cream, or ointment and cover it lightly.
- Keep the patient from scratching the area.
- Watch for intensifying redness, tenderness, or the surface of the skin heating up. These are all signs of infection.
- If infection develops or if the rash doesn't go away, seek medical attention.

POISONOUS PLANT IDENTIFICATION

www.webmd.com

Poison ivy, oak, and sumac, and a few other plants which we won't discuss here are all poisonous plants that can have adverse effects Contact Dermatitis) on human skin. All of these plants contain an oil called urushiol. Contact between this oil and your skin usually causes an itchy, blistering rash that spreads when you scratch the affected area.

POISON IVY

Poison ivy comes in two configurations, a vine or a shrub. Poison ivy has a leaf consisting of three pointed leaflets; the center leaflet is longer than the ones on either side. The edges of the leaflets are usually smooth or toothed, but are sometimes lobed. The leaves range in size from a third of an inch to a shade over two inches in length. When they sprout in the spring they appear reddish. During the summer they turn leaf green, and in the autumn they turn assorted shades of yellow, orange, or red. At the main stem close to where the leaflets converge, small greenish flowers grow in bunches. Even later in the season, clusters of poisonous, berrylike seeds that have a whitish, waxy look form where the flowers were.

Poison Oak

Poison oak is a deciduous shrub that can be found anywhere in North America that has an elevation under five thousand feet. It generally presents as a climbing vine roots that attach to the trunks of sycamore and oak trees. Poison oak can also present in the form of dense undergrowth in chaparral and coastal sage scrub. The leaves, much like Poison Ivy, generally have three leaflets (though some have as many as five), the terminal one on a slender stalk. Eastern poison ivy usually has a longer stalk and the leaflet margins tend to be less serrated (less "oak-like.) New growth and autumn leaves often turn bright shades of pink and red.

POISON SUMAC

Poison Sumac grows in peat bogs and swamps. It is a woody year round shrub or small tree that grows from five to twenty-five feet tall.

Poison Sumac has a fruit that grows between the leaf and the branch. It has about seven to thirteen leaflets shaped in a feather-like arrangement with the leaves arrayed in an alternating pattern on the vine. The foliage changes to brilliant orange or scarlet colors in the autumn.

LAND NAVIGATION

TO MOVE OR NOT TO MOVE

The cardinal rule of survival is 'use your head.' The first question you need to ask yourself is whether it is wiser to stay where you are or make an effort to walk out. If you are the survivor of the crash of an aircraft, don't move. Rescue operations will be searching for the wreckage, not combing the wilderness for survivors. If your location is known to friends and relatives, you are probably safer to stay where you are.

If you need to walk out, you absolutely have to have some knowledge of the area. It doesn't help to know in which direction North lies if you have no idea of the location of the roads in the area, and where they lead to. Even if you have the latest in lensatic compasses in your survival kit, without a detailed topographical map the compass is serious overkill. We will proceed on the assumption that you know in which direction you need to travel and simply need to know where magnetic North is. The stories you were told as a child about moss only growing on the

North side of a tree are entirely untrue. Determining the basic directions is very simple and can be determined by a number of simple methods. We will deal with three of the simplest methods here, the Shadow Tip Method, the Watch Method, and Celestial Navigation.

SHADOW TIP METHOD

1 Mark the shadow's tip.

2 Mark the new position
   and draw a line through
   the two marks.

3 Stand with the first mark to
   your left and the second
   mark to your right—you are
   now facing north.

danger.mongabay.com

The Shadow Tip method is extremely simple. All
you require is a level spot in the sunshine, a stick
about a yard long and two distinctive items to mark

the tip of the stick's shadow on the ground. Drive the stick perpendicular to the ground and mark the top of its shadow by marking the dirt or placing a marker on the ground. This mark will always indicate west, no matter where on Earth you are located. Wait a minimum of fifteen minutes and then mark the shadow's tip again in the same manner as before. Draw a line from the first marker to the second marker. This line, with the first marker to your left, is the East-West line. Perpendicular to this line is the North-South line, with North being straight ahead and West (the first mark) to your left.

THE WATCH METHOD

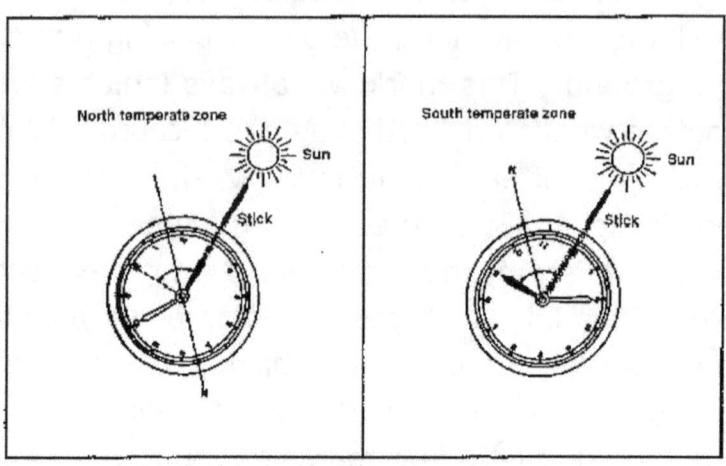

Figure 2-2, Using a watch to find north.

In order to make the watch method work, you must make certain that your watch is not set on daylight savings time. Hold your watch flat in your hand and point the hour hand directly towards the sun. Looking at the face of the watch, bisect the angle created by the hour hand and the 12 on the watch face and you will establish your north-south baseline. Check the sun to determine whether it is in the East (before noon) or in the West (afternoon), then orient yourself to where your left shoulder is facing West. Straight ahead will be north. If you have a digital watch, simply draw the current time on a watch face on paper and use it just as you would a watch. This only works in the Northern Hemisphere. In the Southern Hemisphere, point the 12 o'clock mark at the sun and bisect the angle between it and the hour hand to get the North-South Baseline.

CELESTIAL NAVIGATION

survivalcommonsense.com

In our case, Celestial Navigation means nothing more than locating the North Star. The axis of the Earth is pointed almost directly at the North Star, or Polaris, and therefore it never seems to move. Polaris is the last star in the handle of Ursa Minor, commonly called the 'Little Dipper'.

The 'Little Dipper can always be located by using the front two stars of the 'Big Dipper', which is probably the easiest of all the celestial signs to recognize. Extend a line through the front two stars of the familiar 'Big Dipper' and you have what amounts to an arrow pointing at Polaris.

WEAPONS AND TOOLS

We need to take a moment here to discuss a matter that seems to be a major issue for modern "survivalists." What do you really need to hunt with, to provide protection for you and your family in today's world? The answer will disappoint a large number of you, but my answer is the result of many late night discussions with men who use guns and knives for their intended purpose every single day of their lives. Soldiers and Police Officers who know their business...and of this I am absolutely certain because they were still alive when I talked with them. These are men who have been at the cutting edge of wars, conflicts, and some of the meanest streets in the world, U.S. Army Rangers, Special Forces, and Police Officers from across the U.S. The basic considerations are:

- What do I need to kill?

- How easy will it be to keep ammunition for it?

- How hard would it be for my 9 year old daughter to use if I was incapacitated?

GUNS

SELECTION

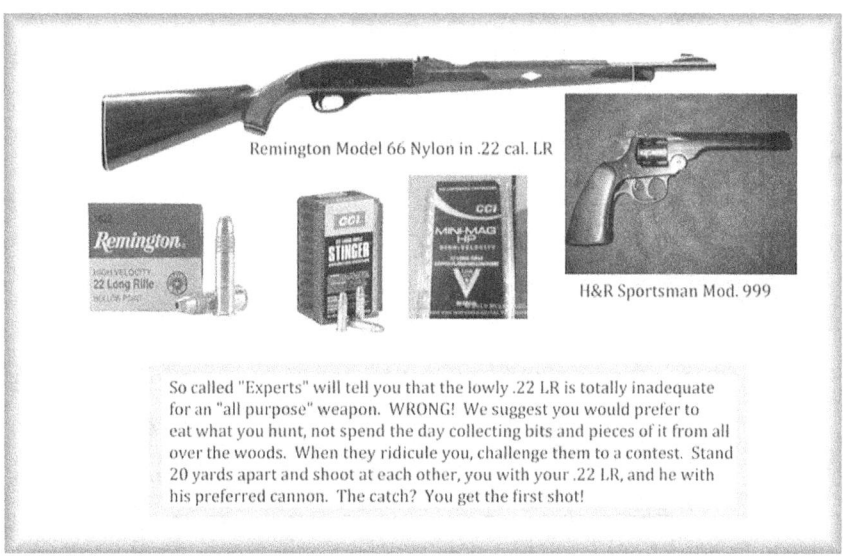

Remington Model 66 Nylon in .22 cal. LR

H&R Sportsman Mod. 999

So called "Experts" will tell you that the lowly .22 LR is totally inadequate for an "all purpose" weapon. WRONG! We suggest you would prefer to eat what you hunt, not spend the day collecting bits and pieces of it from all over the woods. When they ridicule you, challenge them to a contest. Stand 20 yards apart and shoot at each other, you with your .22 LR, and he with his preferred cannon. The catch? You get the first shot!

Considering the nature of this subject and the intense feelings of shooter this ought to be a controversial subject...but it isn't really. Hunters, soldiers, law enforcement officers, and just plain gun nuts will sit and endlessly debate the merits of a particular gun or caliber that they favor. Remember that each group has a particular purpose that they use these tools (and that is what they are, nothing more and nothing less,) for. So what is the logical choice for the average person?

The answer is really pretty simple really. The .22 caliber long rifle will handle any chore you assign it unless you live in bear country. You can sit around and talk stopping power, knockdown, any subject you like, but the final answer is...one .22 round in the left eye of a malcontent will kill him deader than thirty rounds fired wildly over his head with an M-16. You can buy .22 rounds in five pound cans, a lifetime supply could be stored in the trunk of your car. You can buy hollow points, Mini Mags, and CCI Stingers. With proper shot placement, these will bring down anything except the largest game. When your buddies start to rag you about your "baby" gun, remind them of a few hard facts. While the M-16 5.56 military round has more powder, its caliber is .223. More homicides are committed each year with the .22 long rifle than with all military calibers combined...they are lethal when used correctly. The .22 long rifle will travel more than a mile before it stops. Stop and think for a moment: in one afternoon you can easily teach your nine year old daughter to shoot like an expert. These guns also have the virtue of being so common that tracing one is virtually impossible, and that makes them hard to confiscate.

CLEANING

Keeping guns clean is essential to their proper functioning...vitally important if you are living off what you hunt. Kits are commercially available at reasonable prices, but the components are readily available and inexpensive. A cleaning kit should contain a minimum of the following:

- Powder solvent
- Oil or gun lubricant
- Brass brush the size of the bore in your gun.
- Toothbrush.
- Soft cloth.

STORING

Any gun should be kept away from unsupervised children and the curious. Emotional arguments aside, a gun is a tool. Like any other tool, it should be treated with respect for the damage it can cause and should always be stored in a protective casing at a minimum, or locked in a gun safe at best. Guns should be stored in a dry environment and sheltered from the elements. When it is being used frequently, such as in a survival situation, it is critical that you keep it lightly coated with oil.

EDGED WEAPONS AND TOOLS

KNIVES

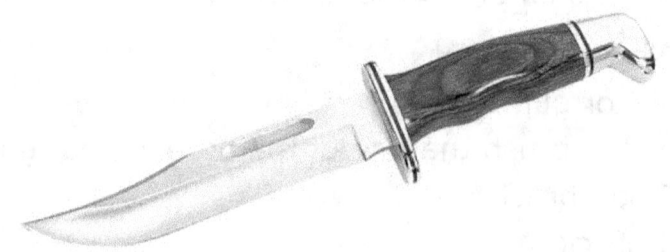

Buck Knives 0119 Special Fixed Blade Knife

A knife will be your most practical and often used tool. Make sure you buy a quality fixed blade knife with a sturdy sheath and a good blade guard. I cannot tell you how many hunting trips, field training exercises, and actual combat missions have been aborted because someone's hand slipped down off the handle onto the blade of a razor sharp knife. You have work to do, you won't have time to heal...

My personal favorite is Buck Knives 0119 Special Fixed Blade Knife, - made in the USA solid knife with Buck Forever Warranty.

MACHETES

Full Tang Fixed Blade Kukri Machete

The machete can be used to cut through forest, undergrowth, and for a variety of cutting and chopping tasks. They generally are less than eighteen inches in length, having a fairly thin blade. It can be used for other tasks, such as butchering large game or cutting food into pieces much like a cleaver is used. It is a handy cutting tool whether you are cooking or clearing an area for a shelter.

As with any tool, you should choose carefully when you select your machete. Keep in mind that you usually get what you pay for, and a quality machete won't come cheap.

The longer and more slender the blade, the more likely your machete blade is to bend or become malformed. The weight of the blade is also a factor in your decision. If you are going to be chopping down trees or firewood, you will want a heavier blade than if your primary use is clearing your way through a jungle; a heavy blade will tire you out very quickly if you're trudging through triple canopy jungle.

I have developed a preference for the curved blades because they tend to hold their shape and their edge better.

HATCHETS AND AXES

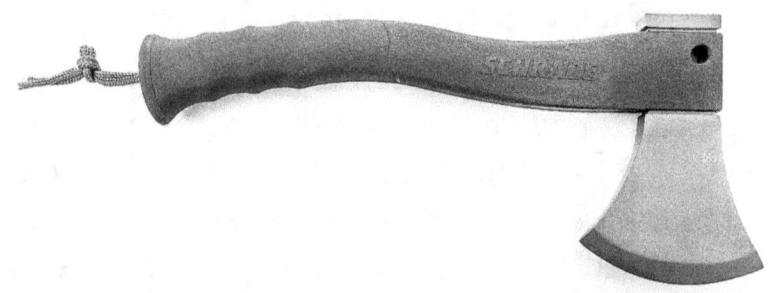

Schrade Axe

Hatchets and axes are useful tools, but keep in mind that the hatchet by its very nature and size is an unwieldy instrument and very difficult to control. I don't have any figures to back my opinion up, but many years of experience tell me that more family camping trips have been abruptly terminated due to hatchet accidents than for any other reason.

Any tool must be used carefully and wisely, but unless you have extensive experience with a hatchet I would recommend against them, especially if you have young children. An axe is a handy tool to have if you're intending to build a large structure such as a log cabin, but you need to evaluate your requirements carefully before you add one to your tool kit.

BOWS

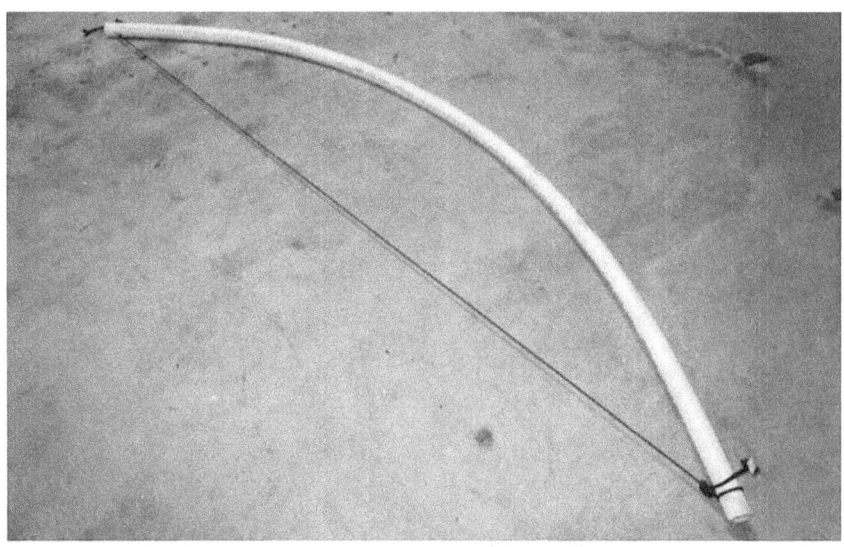

www.survivalexposed.com

Bows are effective hunting weapons, but they are primitive and difficult for the beginner to master. Arrows tend to get lost or their points and fletching become damaged with use. If you are caught without a weapon and you need to construct a primitive weapon, a bow can be a lifesaver, but if you have a choice, stick to the less primitive weapons. The illustration above shows how a simple survival bow can be constructed using PVC pipe and cordage.

SHOVEL/ENTRENCHING TOOL

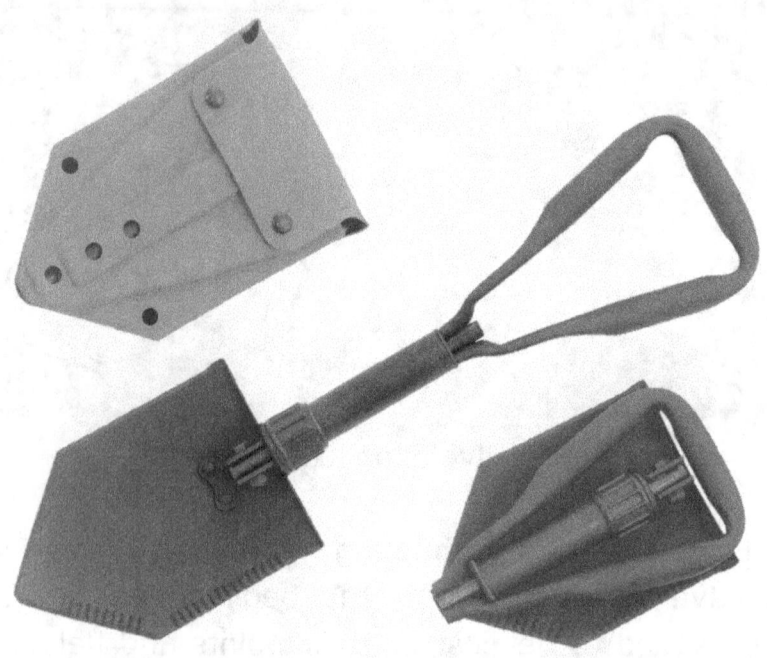

Tri-Fold Entrenching Tool

No matter what situation you find yourself in, a shovel of some sort is an absolute necessity in a survival setting. There are an infinite number of options available when selecting a shovel for any survival situation, but in my mind there is only one real choice. The U.S. military style entrenching tool can serve as a shovel, an axe, a saw, or a weapon. It is equally handy for digging a sanitary facility or chopping down a small tree. From personal experience, I can testify that it is a formidable weapon in close combat.

One of the best things about the entrenching tool is that it is incredibly strong even though it folds up small enough to fit in a pouch and be carried on your belt. The total weight of the entrenching tool is about three pounds. Note the serrated edge which can be used as a saw.

CLIMBING

Climbing and rappelling are skills that are often overlooked when people think of what it might take to get by after a disaster, but in many cases these skills can mean the difference between a happy outcome and a tragedy. Over the long term, these skills are not only useful in emergencies, but could even be essential maintenance wise in getting things back to normal. Windmills, water towers, roofs will all need maintenance, and bridges will have to be repaired as well.

The skills you learn in climbing have other purposes as well. A knowledge of ropes and knots is essential in building primitive shelters, making a travois to haul heavy loads or injured people, or constructing stretchers, swings, hammocks, and other items for your use or comfort. We need to start with a discussion about ropes and cords.

ROPES AND CORDS

NYLON LAID ROPE

Solid Braided Nylon Rope

Ropes and cords are the most critical pieces of climbing equipment. They provide fall protection for both climbers and equipment in the course of steep climbs or descents. They can also be used to secure equipment or to transport it. Up through the 1980's, climbers normally used 7/16" nylon laid rope for climbing and rappelling.

KERNMANTLE ROPE

Singing Rock R44 NFPA Static Rope

Since kernmantle ropes were introduced, they have generally replaced the old nylon laid rope because of their additional strength and abrasion resistance. Kernmantle ropes are covered with a smooth sheath covering a braided or woven core of nylon rope strands. Laid ropes are still used because they are less costly, but they are no longer recommended for use where rope failure might cause injury or the loss of equipment. There are two types of kernmantle rope:

- Dynamic, which is used for climbing, stretches by eight to twelve percent of its length under a load. The elasticity is necessary to reduce the impact force on the climber and associated equipment such as anchors in the event of a fall.

- Static, which is circumstances where elasticity is undesirable, such as when a very heavy static load is placed on the rope. Static ropes should never be used for climbing, because even a fall of a few feet could create enough impact force to cause injury to both the climber and belay man, or cause the anchor to fail.

CARING FOR ROPES AND GEAR

ROPES

Ropes in daily use should be replaced once a year. A rope used only occasionally can be used for four to five years provided it is kept clean and abrasion free.

- Never step on a rope or drag it on the ground any more than absolutely necessary.
- Never run your rope over a sharp or rough edge. Pad the suspect edges with heavy cloth to protect the rope.
- Inspect your ropes carefully before, during, and after each use, checking meticulously for cuts, frayed spots, soft or worn spots, mildew, and abrasions.
- Keep all ropes away from oils, acids, and other materials that might degrade the rope.
- Never run ropes across one another under tension. The friction generated will cause heat that can damage the rope.
- Don't leave ropes under tension or knotted when they are not in use.

- When cleaning rope, use cool water, and then coil it loosely, and don't place it in direct sunlight to dry. Artificial fibers are easily damaged by exposure to ultraviolet radiation. Never use heat to dry a freshly cleaned rope.

SLINGS

Slings are loops of rope, cord, or webbing. The uses for these loops are virtually limitless. They constitute an essential link between the climber, the rope, the carabiners, and the anchors. They are rarely hand-made; usually they are purchased from and certified by the manufacturer.

CARABINERS

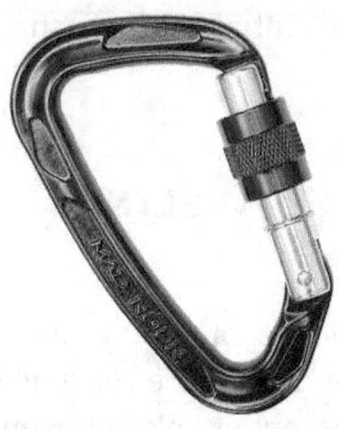

Mad Rock Super Tech Screw Carabiner

The carabiner is a metal loop having a spring-loaded gate, and is used to connect other components together quickly and reversibly. This simple metal loop is the critical connection between the climber and the rope. Manufacturers use newer metal alloys that are much lighter than steel while retaining their tensile strength, and climbers generally suspend several from a sling and carry them along on the climb. Basic carabiners come in a variety of shapes and sizes, and the ones you select depend greatly on your needs and preferences.

PROTECTION

Figure 10-1. EXAMPLES OF TRADITIONAL (REMOVABLE) PROTECTION USED ON ROCK

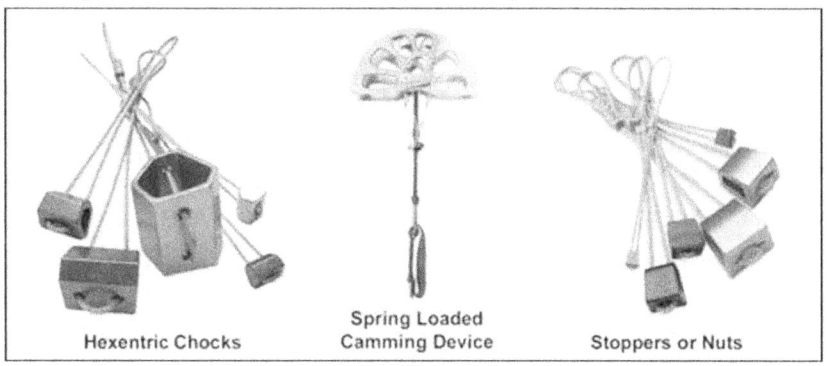

Hexentric Chocks   Spring Loaded Camming Device   Stoppers or Nuts

Figure 10-2. EXAMPLES OF FIXED (PERMANENT OR SEMI) PROTECTION USED ON ROCK

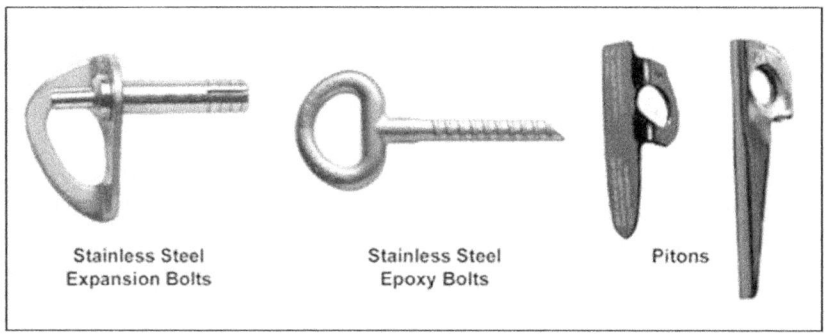

Stainless Steel Expansion Bolts   Stainless Steel Epoxy Bolts   Pitons

SH 21-76 UNITED STATES ARMY RANGER HANDBOOK
JULY 2006 Edition

"Protection", in climbing terminology, is any piece of gear used to construct an anchor. Protection should not be confused with the anchor itself, which can be formed by several pieces of protection, and can subsequently hold the entire weight of the lifeline. Protections, climber, belayer, and ropes, form the lifeline of the climbing team. The rope ties the two climbers together, and the protection connects them to the surface they are traversing. The two types of artificial protection are traditional (removable) and fixed (usually permanent.)

ANCHORS

An anchor is the tie off point for your climbing rope, and it has to be strong enough to support any load you place on the rope. Usually the anchor is a tree or a post, but you can use several pieces of artificial or natural protection together to make a multipoint anchor. Anchors are classified as either artificial or natural:

- Artificial anchors are made from man-made materials such as carabiners, pitons, clamps, and slings.
- Natural Anchors such as trees, shrubs, and boulders are the most common anchors. The only requirements for a natural anchor are that you must be able to tie your rope around it and it has to be able to support the weight of the load.

BASIC KNOTS

Knots are essential to everyone, and not just for climbing. The ability to tie different types of knots is essential for primitive construction, securing loads, making bundles, and a myriad of daily tasks. The following knots should provide you with a large enough repertoire to cover most situations you might encounter.

SQUARE KNOT

Figure 10-5. SQUARE KNOT

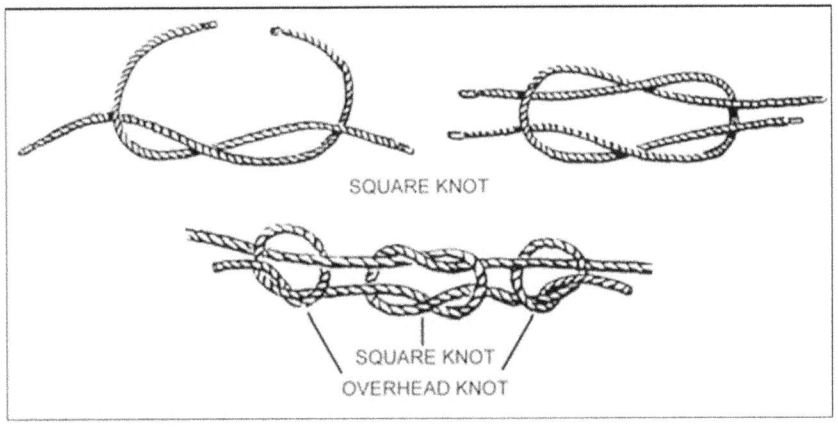

SQUARE KNOT

SQUARE KNOT
OVERHEAD KNOT

SH 21-76 UNITED STATES ARMY RANGER HANDBOOK
JULY 2006 Edition

The square knot is used to join two ropes together. It works best when joining two pieces of equal diameter, but it will work if the ropes are not the same size. The square knot has two interlinking bights, or loops, the running ends of which exit on the same side of the standing end of the rope. The short tails (should be about four inches long) left after connecting the two ropes should be secured by tying an overhand knot on the standing end.

ROUND-TURN WITH TWO HALF HITCHES

Figure 10-6. ROUND-TURN WITH TWO HALF-HITCHES

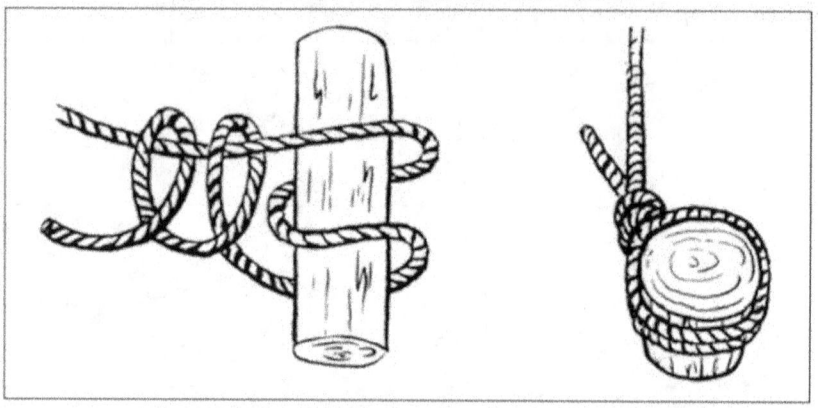

SH 21-76 UNITED STATES ARMY RANGER HANDBOOK
JULY 2006 Edition

This is a quick and easy constant tension anchor knot. The rope is wrapped around the anchor point one time with both ropes parallel, touching, and not crossing. The half hitches have to be tightly dressed against the round turn, with the trailing end sticking out the top of the last half-hitch. Leave at least a four inch tail on the working end.

END-OF-THE-ROPE CLOVE HITCH

This is a transitional anchor knot that has to have constant tension applied to make it secure. Make two wraps around the anchor without crossing them and leaving no more than one rope width between the wraps. The trailing end of the rope should extend four inches past the final half hitch in the opposite direction of the pull.

Figure 10-7. END-OF-THE-ROPE CLOVE HITCH

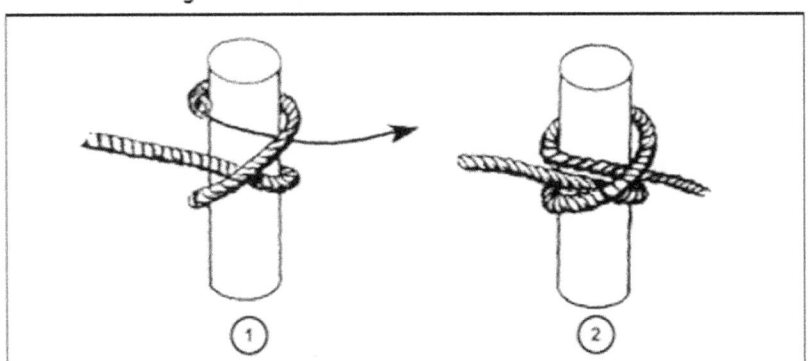

Figure 10-8. MIDDLE-OF-THE-ROPE CLOVE HITCH

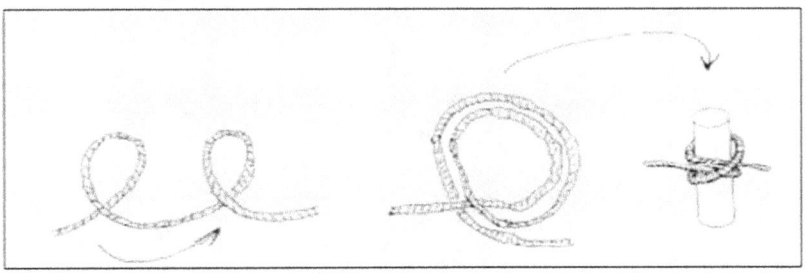

SH 21-76 UNITED STATES ARMY RANGER HANDBOOK
JULY 2006 Edition

MIDDLE OF THE ROPE CLOVE HITCH

This knot is used to tie off the middle of a rope to an anchor. Wrap the rope twice around the anchor leaving no more than one rope width between turns, using one of the wraps as a locking bar to trap the two wraps against the anchor surface. Make sure the locking bar is opposite the direction of pull.

DOUBLE FIGURE EIGHT KNOT

Figure 10-10. DOUBLE FIGURE EIGHT-LOOP KNOT

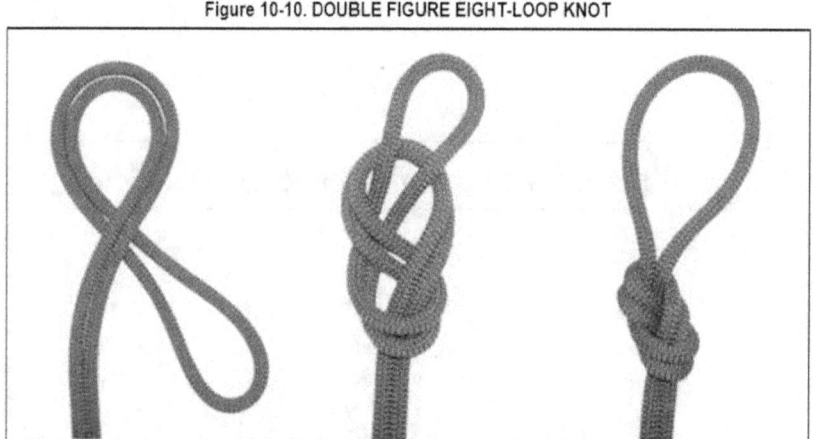

SH 21-76 UNITED STATES ARMY RANGER HANDBOOK
JULY 2006 Edition

Use a Figure Eight loop knot to make a fixed loop in your rope, at the end or anywhere along its length. Figure Eight loop knots are formed looping the rope into the shape of a Figure Eight without twisting it, leaving a finished loop at least large enough to insert a carabiner. If you form the knot at the terminal end of a rope, leave at least a four inch tail.

REROUTED FIGURE EIGHT KNOT

Figure 10-11. REROUTED FIGURE EIGHT KNOT

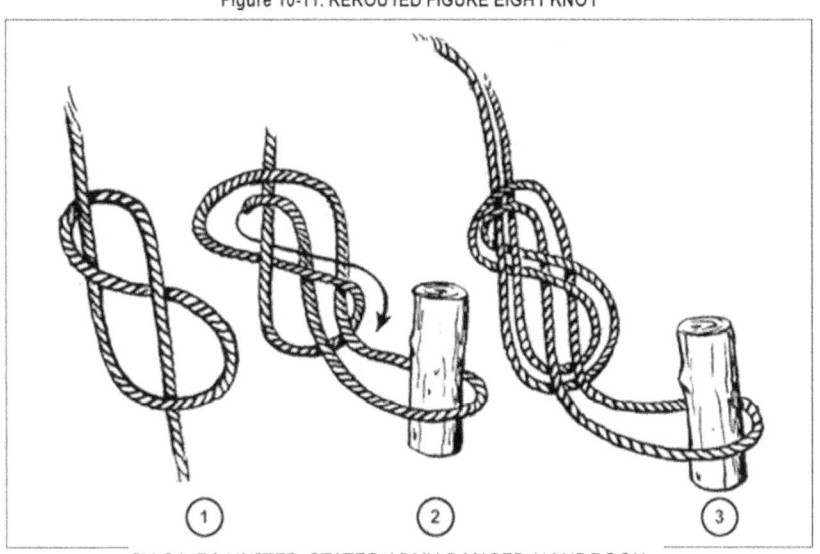

SH 21-76 UNITED STATES ARMY RANGER HANDBOOK
JULY 2006 Edition

This anchor knot can also be used to attach the rope to a fixed anchor. Make a simple Figure Eight in your rope and pass the working end around your anchor. Reroute the working end back through to form a double Figure Eight being careful not to twist the rope. Leave at least a four inch tail on the working end.

RAPPEL SEAT

Black Diamond Momentum Climbing Harness

A rappel seat is a harness used to support your body when you rappel or climb.

It can also be used when you are working in trees or when working at heights. The rappel seat or "Swiss Seat" can be tied for use by either left handed or right handed climbers. The leg straps are tight, not crossed, and they are centered on buttocks. The leg straps form locking half hitches around the rope at the waist. Use a square knot tied on the right hip (opposite hip for left handers) and finish off the square knot with two overhand knots. The tails need to be even and no more than six inches long. When you have finished tying your seat, insert a carabiner around all ropes (front and center), with the gate opening up and away. The carabiner may not contact the square or the overhand knot. When tied properly, you cannot insert your fist between your body and the harness.

BELAYS

Belaying is any technique used to create tension and slow or stop the fall of the individual on the rope. The belayer can also help in controlling your rate of descent, and it is his job to manage the running end of the rope so that the climber/rapeller doesn't get tangled in it. The belay man absolutely must solidly anchored to so that he doesn't get tugged out of his position and lose control of the rope. There are two ways a belay man can do this:

BODY BELAY

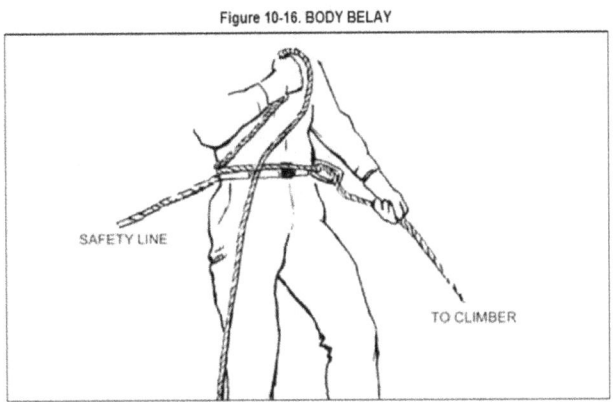

Figure 10-16. BODY BELAY

SAFETY LINE

TO CLIMBER

SH 21-76 UNITED STATES ARMY RANGER HANDBOOK
JULY 2006 Edition

This consists of using your body to apply friction by stringing the rope around your body and using a closing motion with your arm across your chest and leaning back against the rope. This will cause friction between the carabiner and the rope, bringing the descending rapeller to a halt. Be prepared, because this will cause the entire weight of the load to be placed on your body.

MECHANICAL BELAY

Figure 10-17. MECHANICAL BELAY

SH 21-76 UNITED STATES ARMY RANGER HANDBOOK
JULY 2006 Edition

This technique uses one of a variety of mechanical devices to assist in controlling the climber's rate of descent.

These techniques and devices absolutely have to be practiced *before* you find yourself needing them. There are a number of excellent training videos on Youtbe.com. This is the URL for one of the better ones:

https://www.youtube.com/watch?v=hetZSbO3tTA

BUILDING A SURVIVAL KIT

There is no way for me to emphasize just how important it is to have a survival kit stashed somewhere convenient in your home, and that everyone in your household knows where it is.

Being prepared doesn't just mean having the supplies you may need in the event of a catastrophic event no one can have absolutely everything they need, that would literally be impossible. Building your kit involves some serious thinking about what items would be the hardest to come by post-event. Considerations would be what type of climate you live in, whether you live in an urban area where stores are nearby or a rural environment where there are none. Are there substantial medical facilities and personnel nearby, or do you need to invest in an expensive First Aid kit and some advanced training? Is there a source of fresh running water nearby, or do you need to focus on water purification techniques? What it boils down to is this: there is no one list of absolutes. Types, quality, and quantity of items you need are dependent in large part on what you will need to survive in *your* environment and in *your* circumstances.

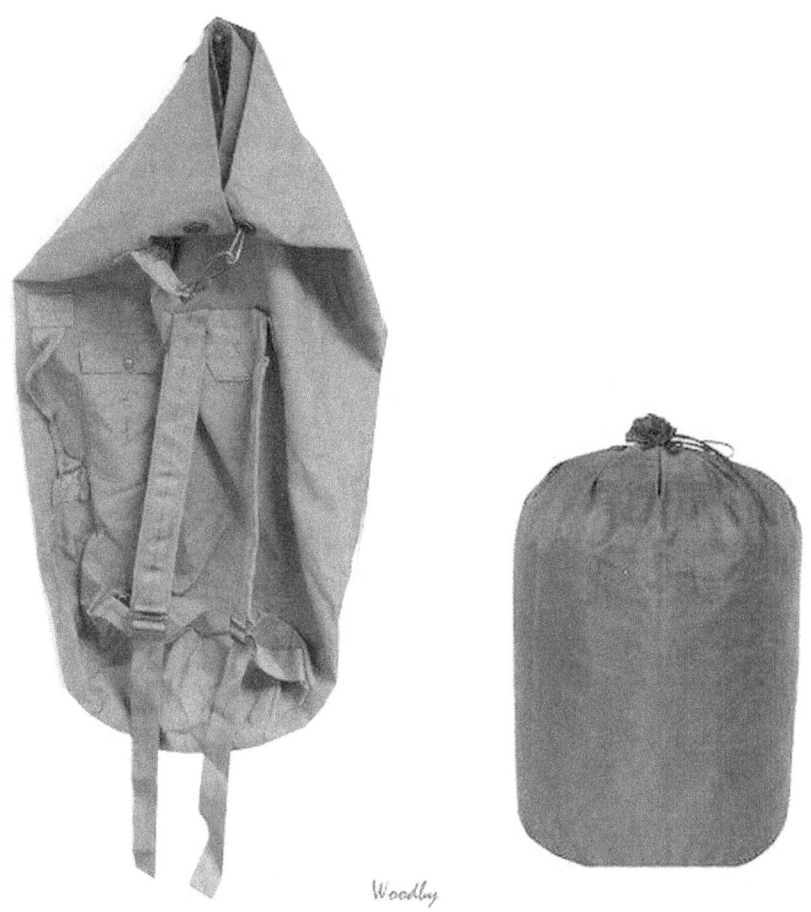

Woodby

You should store equipment and supplies in a portable, easy-to-carry survival/catastrophe kit that you can use at home or carry with you if you have to evacuate. I use a couple of U.S. Army surplus duffel bags (pictured below.) They are readily available, durable, inexpensive, and have back straps that make them easier to carry...and packed correctly, they can contain an enormous number of items. They can be easily stored in a hall closet and easily carried if you have to leave your home in a hurry.

Recommendations for content:

- Water: purchase gallon jugs, they are cheaper and can be stacked in boxes beside your kit. Quantity dependent on your location, but I recommend you keep a three day supply if you have to leave your home.
- Matches, butane lighters, charcoal lighters, and/or a fire starting kit
- Food: Canned goods, dried foods, powdered baby formula, and other non-perishable items that require little in the way of preparation. Again, keep a supply dependent on your location and circumstances.
- Knife
- Entrenching tool
- Guns and ammunition
- Manual or battery operated can opener
- Flashlights and candles
- NOAA Weather Radio
- Spare batteries
- First Aid Kit, prescription medications, medical supplies such as insulin syringes, spare glasses

or contact lenses, hearing aids with extra batteries. You will also need a medication list and personal medical information.
- Personal hygiene items such as toothbrushes and paste, toilet paper, and sanitary napkins.
- Emergency blankets and sleeping bags
- Map of the area
- Two-way radios
- Spare set of car and house keys
- Copies of personal documents (proof of address, deed/lease to home, passports, birth certificates, insurance policies)

Some additional items you might keep on hand:

- Cell phones with chargers
- Rain gear
- Towels
- Work gloves
- Tools/supplies for securing your home
- Spare clothing and shoes
- Plastic sheeting
- Duct tape
- Liquid bleach

Use your mind and your imagination. Don't leave out anything you imagine you might need that will still fit inside your duffle bag.

URBAN SURVIVAL

Much of what is written about survival assumes a wilderness survival situation. There are several advantages to trying to survive in the wild; primarily the advantage of not having to worry about all the strangers around you and making the necessary adjustments to get them to fit into your group. On top of that, you don't have the burden of sharing the available resources that man and nature have provided for you.

In an urban survival setting, your problem is reversed. Large numbers of total strangers will be competing with you for limited resources. Even so, the urban setting is the one most of us are likely to be facing when the time comes. Fundamental skills like the ones we have already been discussing can be useful even in the city, but they don't address many of the problems you will encounter in an urban setting.

While some survival skills, like purifying water and starting a fire are universal, there are many other skills which are critical for an urban survival situation. Many of those skills affect how we deal with the other people around us, specifically protecting ourselves and our families from them. There are also some skills which are specific to a financial collapse, which may not be as important in the aftermath of other disasters. From here on out, we're going to address the skills peculiar to urban survival situations.

Survivalists are looked upon by our society as "eccentric", so many survivors of a natural catastrophe are going to be totally unprepared for the aftermath of a catastrophic event. In an urban setting, many won't have what they need...but they may well have something that *you* need. Those shared needs establish the basis for a new type of economy, which will be desperately needed since the economy we have is based more on computers and electronics more than on cash. No more banks, no more credit cards, no more electronic funds transfers...all these things lead us to the most basic commerce system of all, the barter system. I have something you need and you have something I need or want, giving us the foundation for a trade. Barter is how our ancestors got by, and it is how we will get by should the need arise.

Communications are likely to be limited, and they will be sorely needed in order to be able to locate practitioners with professional skills that we will be acutely short of, such as advanced medical care, dentistry, and other things. In all likelihood there won't be any cell towers or people to keep the telecommunications systems up and running...and even if we did, it's highly unlikely that we will have power to run them and charge up our batteries. Considering this possibility, we'll conduct a short discussion on building a radio transmitter/receiver.

The most dangerous predators you will be facing won't be lions and tigers and bears, it will be other humans. You can bet that there are plenty of people who made no advance preparations for a major disaster, and they will be out in drives, desperate to have what you in your wisdom have laid by for just such an emergency. When they are unable to locate food for their families, they will become predators, seeking to take by force what they need and do not have. You must be able to defend yourself and your family from these two legged predators, so we will take a look at self-defense.

We're going to take a look at basic mechanical maintenance and repair so that we can keep those machines we have or the ones we will need in running condition.

A look at plumbing principles is going to be necessary, both indoor and outdoor. We'll have a look at adaptability, teaching, firefighting, and electricity. There will also be a discussion about advanced medical care training, along with a discussion of many other things that are simply common sense. Last of all, we're going to discuss something really vital...a reading list of books you will need to find either before or after the catastrophic event.

Keep in mind that the more skills you have already developed, the greater your chances are for survival. Those skills will also come in handy to barter or trade for goods and services that are hard to come by. In other words, even if the economy is tanked to hell, if you have skills, you have a job.

MONEY AND BARTER

In the event of a large scale disaster, we could reasonably anticipate a total collapse of our infrastructure. As time passes with no sign of things returning to normal, we can expect to see that the paper money and coins we use now will become worthless. When people realize that without a government and an electronic means of banking, money will cease to have value as a medium of commerce. Once money is no longer of any real value, people will begin to try to purchase items with time honored valuables like gems and precious metals, and then with trade goods or barter items

Barter items are of value even in normal circumstances, but they will be the gold standard after a major catastrophic event. Trade will once again mean precisely that. If you have access to gasoline and your neighbor doesn't have any, he will trade canned goods, purified water, clothing, and whatever he has that you might need in exchange for your gasoline. It will be up to the two of you to determine the items' relative value and establish how much each of you is willing to trade for what items...and it is up to you to determine what items might be of the greatest value based upon your geographic location and the resources available close by. Shortages are going to occur, and if you correctly anticipate what those might be and arrange to have or locate a stockpile of them, you will become a well-to-do survivor.

What commodities are likely to be in short supply? Unquestionably foodstuffs with high caloric and or high carbohydrate values, water and containers to hold it, alcohol, First Aid supplies such as aspirin and other pain killers, anti-biotic pills and ointment are great choices and relatively easy to stockpile. Lighters and lighter fluid or fuel, matches, firearms and ammunition, and batteries are other superior choices.

Plant seeds for vegetable gardens, clothing items such as socks, sweatshirts, and sweat pants will be useful and therefore valuable. I'm not suggesting that you build up inventory like a store would have, just try to keep in mind that things you know you will need for your family's survival will also be of value to others.

The idea is not to try and stock a retail store, just realize that what may be important to your survival is also important of others facing the same commodities shortage. The value of everything you own and are able to salvage will be redefined in a new set of circumstances. Try to take advantage of that.

COMMUNICATIONS

SIMPLE RADIO RECEIVER

A crystal radio set is the most primitive type of radio. It is built of simple, common components that can be found almost anywhere, even lying around the house, and is amazingly easy to construct. A crystal radio does not need batteries or any other power source, but it will still receive radio transmissions in the AM band.

Components:

- A 16 oz. sturdy plastic bottle, five to seven inches in length. A toilet paper tube or a cardboard oatmeal container can be substituted for the bottle.)
- Fifty feet of 22-18 gauge enamel-coated (copper) magnet wire.
- One germanium diode. (1N34A diode, Radio Shack part number 276-1123).
- A telephone handset.
- A few sets of alligator jumper clips.
- Fifty to one hundred feet of stranded, insulated wire for an antenna.

Once you've acquired your materials and put them on a flat and well lit work surface, take an icepick or an awl and poke two holes half an inch apart close to the top of the bottle. Make two similar holes near the bottom of the bottle. Make an effort to make the holes just wide enough to insert the wires.

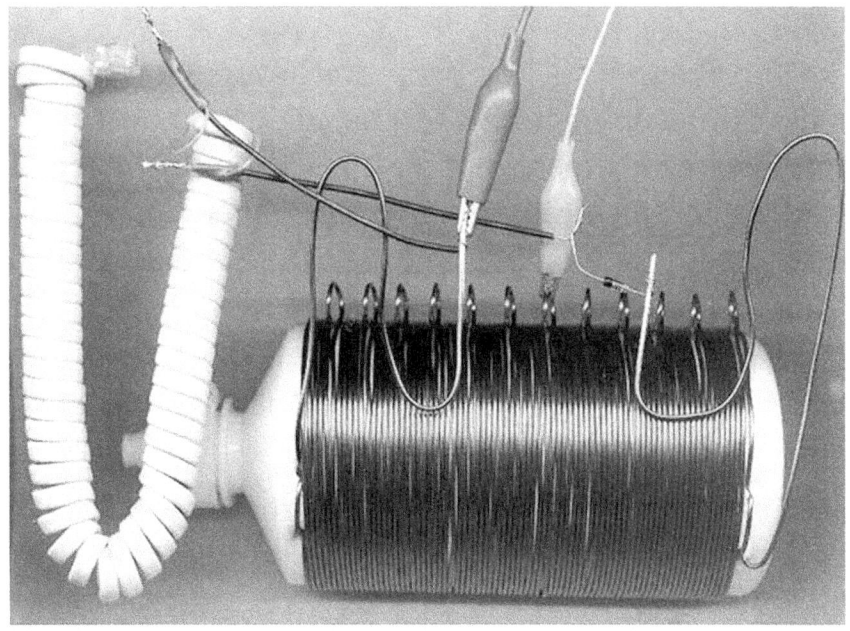

http://www.iseeidoimake.com/

Insert the copper wire in through the top holes and leave about eight inches of wire out. Then take long end of the wire and wrap it around the bottle five times keeping each warp tight against the previous wrap. At this time, stop and wrap the wire around a pencil or pen a single time to make a loop, leaving the pencil or pen in place for the time being.

Wrap the copper wire around the bottle five more times and make another loop. Continue down the length of the bottle, adding another loop every five wraps until the bottle is completely covered down to the second set of holes at the other end. Measure off another eight inches of the coated wire and cut it, then thread the extra eight inches through the two holes.

Take the pencil (or pen, whichever you used to make the loops) out and set it aside. Using an emory board or sandpaper, remove the coating at the end of the eight inch tail. Use the sandpaper to strip the insulation from the ends of the coated wire as well as from the loops you made with the pen or pencil. If the wire you used was vinyl coated, either pinch the coating with your fingernails and pull the coating or use a knife. (Strip the insulation.)

Solder the germanium diode to the bottom wire if you have the capability, but either twisting the wires together and taping them, or using the alligator jumpers will work...though soldering is the preferred (and best) method.

Take the telephone handset cord and strip off one of the modular connectors. Inside, you will find four wires. If it's not your lucky day, the wires will be all one color, or one will be red and the others will be white. To locate the correct wires, strip off the insulation from the last half inch of each wire, then take a battery (a C, D, or AA cell battery), and touch one wire to plus and another to minus on the battery until you hear a clicking sound in the handset earphone. When the clicking occurs, the two wires touching the battery are the two you want. If it is your lucky day, the wires will be color codes, and you will need to use the yellow and black ones.

Solder (or twist and tape) either the yellow or black wire to your Germanium diode, then use other wire (yellow or black), attaching it to the wire at the top of the bottle.

Open the jaws of one end of one of your alligator jumper clips to one of the loops atop the coil (the wire wrapped bottle) and clip the other end to your antenna wire. Join another alligator clip to the wire at the top of the bottle. The free end of the second alligator clip will need to be attached to something metal that is grounded.

Now you can listen to different radio stations on the telephone handset by the alligator clip from loop to loop on the coil.

A SIMPLE RADIO TRANSMITTER

Note: Consult local, state, and Federal communications laws before building and using any kind of radio transmitter unless you are in a survival situation.

This simple transmitter can be assembled in around ten minutes, and it's small enough to hold in the palm of your hand. It has a limited range, dependent upon the length and height of your antenna wire.

Components:

- A one megahertz crystal clock oscillator like the ones used in computers.
- A 1000 ohm to 8 ohm audio transformer, like Radio Shack part #273-1380.
- A generic general purpose printed circuit board.
- A phone plug that matches the jack in your sound source
- A 9 volt battery clip. Radio Shack has a heavy duty type, part number 270-324.
- A 9 volt battery.
- A set of alligator jumpers that you can purchase anywhere electronics parts are sold.

- Some insulated wire for an antenna; you can even use the antenna wire you used for your receiver.

The oscillator is the core of the transmitter. We will only use three of the four leads on the oscillator. When we hook up the power to two of the leads, the voltage on third lead will jump between 0 volts and 5 volts at a rate of a million times every second.

The bottom left corner of the oscillator's container is sharp instead of rounded like the other corners. The sharp corner has the unused lead. That lead will be used for no other reason than to help hold the can down snugly on the printed circuit board.

The audio transformer is the other major component, and it is used as a modulator in this circuit. It changes the strength of the radio waves to match the loudness of the sound to be transmitted. There are two leads on one side of the transformer and three on the opposite side. The two leads are on the 8 ohm side and the three leads are on the 1000 ohm side. The center lead in the set of three won't be used in this circuit.

In order to get the best range, we put the 8 ohm side of the transformer in series with the oscillator, so the signal source has to be able to drive a heavy load, such as an 8 ohm speaker. If your signal source is weak, like an MP3 player or an iPod (they can only drive a set of 32 ohm earphones,) you will need to reverse the transformer so that the 8 ohm side is connected to the signal source and the 1,000 ohm side is in series with the oscillator. You won't get as much range, but you'll have a better chance of getting some modulation of the signal.

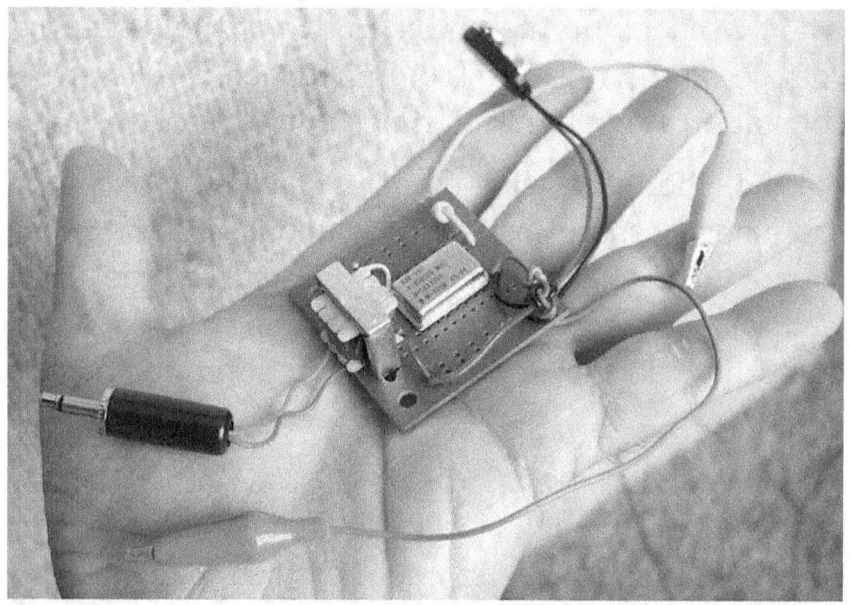

http://sci-toys.com/

Lay out your components on a flat, well lit work surface. Bend the two metal tabs on the bottom of the transformer flat so that you can glue it to the printed circuit board. Secure the transformer to the left side of the printed circuit board, copper side down, leaving ample space on the other side for the oscillator. Insert the oscillator leads into the printed circuit board as far to the right as you can. Carefully bend the oscillator leads over so that it is firmly attached to the circuit board.

Using as little solder as possible (so that it won't form bridges between the copper foil circuits on the circuit board), solder the pins of the oscillator to the copper foil on the circuit board.

The red wire from the transformer needs to be inserted the bottom left hole on the circuit board), and then take the red wire from the battery clip and place it in another unused hole that is connected by printed circuit to the first hole, so that the two red wires complete a circuit. Solder the two wires to the circuit.

Take the white transformer wire and inert it into a hole that is connected to the top left pin of the oscillator by a printed circuit. Solder the wire in place, again using as little solder as possible.

Take one of your alligator clips and cut in half, leaving you two pieces of wire ending in an alligator clip. Remove the insulation from the last half inch of each wire.

Take the black wire from the battery clip and place it into a hole on the circuit board that connects to the bottom right pin of the oscillator. Take one of the alligator clip leads and tuck the stripped end into a hole that is also connected to the bottom right pin of the oscillator, then solder the two wires in place. The alligator clip can then be connected to a solidly grounded piece of metal. The other alligator clip should be placed into a hole connected by printed circuit with the top right pin of the oscillator and soldered in place for your antenna connection.

Open the end of the phone plug, and take the blue and green wires from the transformer inside the plastic handle. Then insert the wires into the small holes in the metal part of the plug and solder them in place. When the metal has cooled down, screw the phone plug back together.

Take the phone plug and insert it into 'audio out' jack on a sound source...a CD player or a tape player, and then attach the 9 volt battery to the battery clip.

Using an AM radio tuned to 1000, place your transmitter nearby so that you can hear your transmission over the radio. The volume controls on both your sound source and on the radio will need to be adjusted for you to get the best sound. The transmitter will only broadcast to a receiver a few inches away until you connect it to your antenna wire, and you'll get better range if you attach the ground wire to a good solid ground.

SELF DEFENSE

For most people, the topic of self-defense conjures up mental images of Bruce Lee, Chuck Norris, Stephen Segall and other, and other famous martial artists leaping through the air and delivering lethal blows and kicks while screaming at the top of their lungs. The reality of self-defense is that true self defense is a matter of keeping calm, avoiding conflict as much as possible, and when it's unavoidable, use whatever means you have at your disposal to end it as quickly as possible. Anger and fear are your most formidable opponents.

SITUATIONAL AWARENESS

Situational Awareness is a term often bandied about by members of various professions, defined within the scope of their particular fields. In terms of self-defense, the phrase to the defender's attentiveness to the details of his attacker(s), his surroundings, and the items or personal characteristics he can use to gain an advantage over his opponent. If you can't get a mental picture of the concept, watch any Jackie Chan movie for some ideas. Virtually any item within reach can be used as a weapon if your wit is quick enough to comprehend this principle. Throwing sand in an opponent's eyes, using a broom to trip him up, using an empty bucket to blind him...all of these things can be summed up by the term "Situational Awareness". Recognize and use absolutely anything within reach to inflict damage, impair your opponent's will and ability to fight, discourage, or distract him. Always keep in mind that unless your opponent is totally committed to your destruction, the best alternative is usually flight.

DETERRENT DEVICES

Generally speaking, there are several devices that you can carry on your person. Below you will find a list of items that could prove very useful in fending off an opponent.

PEPPER SPRAY

SABRE Red Pepper Spray

Pepper Spray is a chemical compound that irritates the eyes, causing tears, pain, and sometimes temporary blindness. It has many purposes, but the commercially available kind is excellent for personal self-defense, even against animals. Its inflammatory effects can cause the eyes to close, frequently causing a temporary blindness that offers defenders an opportunity to escape.

STUN GUNS

An electroshock weapon, a stun gun is a debilitating weapon that temporarily incapacitates either a person or an animal with an electric shock.

VIPERTEK VTS-989 Heavy Duty Stun Gun

There are different types of stun gun:

- An *electroshock gun* conveys the electric shock to your target using a projectile.
- A *directed-energy weapon* discharges energy in a particular direction (chosen by the defender) without using a projectile. Renders the target unconscious.
- A Taser is an electroshock weapon sold by Taser International that propels two small dart-like electrodes connected to the main unit

by conductors into the skin of your opponent. It generates an electric current to interrupt conscious control of the target's muscles, causing strong involuntary muscle contractions.

KEYS

Your key ring is an item which you almost always carry with you, and it makes a surprisingly effective weapon.

The keys can be inserted between your fingers and used as a slashing weapon, it can be used in bulk to make your fist harder, or, if it's large enough, can be used as a striking weapon.

WHATEVER IS AT HAND

Nearly anything you can get your hands on can be used as a weapon. Sticks, stones, sand, ordinary household objects, clothing articles such as shoes or belts. Anything that gives you any kind of advantage at all over your opponent can be used as a weapon. Your *mind,* your *imagination,* is your greatest weapon.

BASIC SELF-DEFENSE

Once again, Youtube.com is an incredible reference for martial arts and self-defense techniques. Many of the videos are produced and directed by true experts in the field, and if a picture is worth a thousand words, a video is worth millions. Watching through a video quickly will tell you if your body is likely to be able to perform the moves the video is trying to teach, and under further review, the video can be reversed and played over and over until you are satisfied that you have mastered the demonstrated technique.

As I stated earlier, keeping your temper and your fear under control is paramount during a hostile encounter. Keep your head, use your mind calmly to determine what steps you will take to defend yourself. Evaluate your adversary and, if applicable, his weapons, and make an informed decision about whether it is wiser to stand and fight or to flee.

Determining where you will strike, how you will strike, and what part of your body you will use to strike depends on the position of your opponent and how close he is to you. Moving closer to your opponent to strike at his nose with your hand is foolish when you're perfectly capable of kicking at his knees, especially is he is larger and stronger than you.

- When you want to strike your adversary on the upper half of his body you will need to use your hand. Strikes can be accomplished with the outer edge of your hand held in a knife hand position, a fist, with the knuckles (fingertips curled under), with rigid fingers extended like a spear head not recommended for the novice), or with the flat of the palms.
- When making strikes to your adversary's eyes, gouge, scratch, or poke at them in order to cause him pain and/or interfere with his sight. Eliminating one of your adversary's advantages adds one to your repertoire. Causing him pain is a distraction that might enable you to escape without harm. A survival fight is not a fight with Marquis of Queensbury rules, it is an attempt to enable you to return to your family uninjured and still able to care for them. Flight under these circumstances should never be considered less than honorable. Think of it as one of the best weapons in your arsenal.
- Your adversary's nose is an excellent target if you can exploit it. The human (and animal) nose is a veritable smorgasbord of nerve endings and injuries to it can cause disorientation, impaired vision, and even death. If your adversary has moved in close, use the heel of your palm to strike up under

his nose. Keep in mind that this is a risky move, it can be lethal if the bones at the top of the nasal cavity are shattered. If you have thrown the whole weight of your body into the move, the splinters can be forced into the brain and cause death. You must strike at least hard enough to make him release you. When an adversary is behind you, you can strike at the cartilage and bones of his nose with your elbows.

- The side of the neck, where both the carotid artery and jugular vein are located, is a larger and easier aiming point. With your fingers extended and joined and your thumb tucked under and slightly bent at the knuckle, you can make an effective strike at your adversary's neck or throat with either the knife edge of your hand or with the tips of your fingers. This move usually just causes pain or stuns your attacker, but if the larynx is crushed by the force of your blow this strike can also be lethal. You can also make this strike with your elbow or forearm.

- One of the easiest and effective targets on your adversary will be his knees, and ideally, this will be the first strike you make. The human knee is one of the largest and most complex joints in the body, and pain or damage to it is debilitating, generally taking away your adversary's ability and his will to fight.

- It is vulnerable from literally every angle and is easy to kick without risk of your foot being grabbed. Kick the side of the knee is likely to cause less injury than kicking the front of the knee. You can cause greater injury kicking the front of the knee, but the injury is less likely to take away his balance. The side-kicks are more likely to remove his ability to maneuver, thus giving you an excellent opportunity to get away from him. This is a situation where it would be great to remember to use anything at hand to debilitate your adversary. Baseball bats, tire irons, and tree limbs can be particularly beneficial in removing your adversary's will to fight.
- Your elbows, knees, and head are the parts of the body that are most painful when hit, but oddly enough, they are also your best and most effective weapons in a fight.
- Defend yourself by using your body and the basic laws of physics. You must use your size, weight, and strength relative to your adversary as a weapon, even if he is larger and stronger than you. That is the basic principle behind Karate, Judo, Kung-Fu, and other martial arts, and it is an essential principle especially when you are smaller than your adversary.
- Never treat a survival fight as you might a bar fight or a playground fight (I'm not an advocate of fighting for any reason other than

the defense of myself or someone else.) Always keep in mind that the choice is between your living to fight another day, or surrendering to the demands of your attacker. If you knock him down, don't wait for him to get up, take him out of the fight. Any kind of strike or punch you deliver needs to have the full weight of your body behind it. Swapping indiscriminate blows toe-to-toe is not where you want to be. When someone attempts to violently assert their will on you, every blow must be planned and designed to injure, debilitate, or to remove your adversary's will to fight (that last is my personal favorite.) Go after his most sensitive body parts, and use the weight of your body to inflict the most damage that you can. Finish it as quickly as you are able to. The best outcome of any fight is that you walk away unscathed.

TECHNIQUES

- When an adversary grabs your wrist, don't try to pull your wrist back. Spread your feet about shoulder width apart (you should always have your feet shoulder width apart and your weight placed on the balls of your feet in any confrontation because it provides you with the balance and mobility to move quickly in any direction), squat down into a strong stance, and then lean forward, bending your elbow in to get out of the wrist hold, then pushing upwards towards his forearm until he can't retain his grip any longer.

- When you are being choked from the front you have a couple of options. The first is to form a spear hand (fingers and thumbs extended and joined, thumb tucked under) and strike straight forward between your adversary's arms, striking him in the throat. Then punch or kick him to get him away from you while he's distracted. The second option would be to clasp your hands together and raise them straight up with all your might, which should break his hold. If that doesn't work, stomp down on his instep with the edge of your foot and repeat the hands clasped arms raised action.

- If you are being choked from behind, stomp down with the edge or heel of your foot on his instep and then strike backwards at his ribs or belly with either of your elbows and move away from him with a twisting motion while his hands are temporarily relaxed.

- If your adversary puts you in a bear hug from behind, first try to strike his nose with the back of your head. If that doesn't work, collapse, leaving him trying to support your entire weight, and try to hit his head with your elbows and stomp the tops of his feet with yours. If all else fails, pry his fingers back, forcing him to release you, and rotate out of his arms, attacking him with your hands, elbows, knees, and feet. Finger prying can also be a successful move in a choke hold.

- If your adversary pins you to the ground, grab onto his wrist with one hand and use your free hand to grasp the back of his elbow, clutching his arm to your chest. Trap his leg by hooking yours over it, then raise your hips and pivot over onto your knees to get on top of him.

SKILLS TO MASTER

There are far too many skills that you need to develop to cover them in depth in a book of this scope and size. I highly recommend that you form a reference library and keep it beside your survival kit. In the event of a disaster or a cataclysmic event, power will more than likely be unavailable, as will access to the internet, making a small reference library a treasure of limitless value.

BASIC VEHICLE MAINTENANCE

Depending on where you are located when disaster strikes, acquiring and maintaining a vehicle should be a relatively easy task. Always pick the newest vehicle or at least one that has been well maintained...those kind are also the most likely to contain an owner's manual in the glove compartment, which will aid you in their maintenance. Always ensure that your personal vehicles have an owner's manual on board as well as a small kit of essential tools.

As a practical matter, everyone in your survival group large enough to operate a motor vehicle should be able to handle basic maintenance skills on any available vehicles. The basic skills you should all be able to handle include:

- Changing a tire.
- Changing the oil.
- Check and maintain the battery.
- Know the difference between gas and diesel and how to refuel the vehicles you have.
- How to use a tow chain or strap.

Once again, the internet is a marvelous resource that will enable you to pick up basic skills that you might need in the event of disaster or catastrophic events. Never before in the history of man has there been such a remarkable learning resource. You should use it often and well, and you should encourage your family members to do the same.

BASIC PLUMBING SKILLS

Understanding plumbing is not really difficult. Water always follows the laws of gravity, and it always follows the path of least resistance.

These days it's no longer necessary to know how to cut and join copper or galvanized piping, PVC replacement parts that mate to existing plumbing are nearly universal and are easily found at even small country hardware stores. Basic plumbing needs can be handled largely with common sense and patience, but a knowledge of the different types of PVC available (did you know that there are different types for hot water and cold water?) and an understanding of what you need to do before applying the glue would be of benefit to any survivor.

Once more, I highly recommend that a basic how to book on simple plumbing should be included in your survival reference library.

UNDERSTANDING ELECTRICITY

Electricity can...strike that...electricity *will* kill you if you don't know what you are doing. Even simple everyday chores like changing a light switch or replacing a fuse can turn deadly in the hands of someone who has no understanding of electricity.

There will be a particular need to understand how to use and maintain a portable generator and how precisely one can be hooked into the service box on a residence. This is another skill that needs to be developed *before* disaster strikes...in many cases you will only get one mistake. A reference book on basic electrical repair is of vital necessity.

BASIC FIREFIGHTING TECHNIQUES

An automobile engine is afire. The electrical service box is gloriously aflame. Little Johnny knocked over a can of hydraulic fluid in the garage and somehow it caught fire.

In terms of fighting these fires, what do the three of them have in common? If you answered that you shouldn't use water to put them out, go to the head of the class. Uncontrolled fire is anathema to our civilization, and once the water pressure disappears from our water systems and the fire trucks stop running, fire is going to be a major issue. Aside from the fact that an unchecked fire will destroy much needed and very scarce resources, the injuries cause by fire are both painful and highly susceptible to infection. Fire can be a killer. A knowledge of fires and methods of controlling them will become a necessity and a responsibility for everyone in a post catastrophe environment. Another reference book!

GARDENING

You can never tell how long local food supplies will hold out...or who might have control over them. With a collapsed economy, a garden full of fresh fruits and vegetables (a sustainable, renewable resource) can not only save your life, it can provide an invaluable source of barter goods. Gardening is simple and inexpensive, and anyone can grow one, even in the city. A reference book on gardening is highly recommended, as well as a small stockpile of seeds!

SURVIVAL TIPS

If you enjoy the weird and the unusual, you're going to love this section. The following are off the wall tips, suggestions, and ideas gleaned from all over the world, and they're in no particular order. Many of them are ingenious, and many of them are actually familiar ideas...but we rarely associate this knowledge with survival situations, even though they will be invaluable to you after a catastrophic or apocalyptic event. I hope you enjoy reading these as much as I enjoyed finding them!

- If for some inexplicable reason you find yourself lost in the center of a desert and have no idea in which direction to travel, simply remember to travel only at night and move in the opposite direction of the path the sun travels in the daytime. The rising and setting of the sun will help you establish that direction. It will be critically important that you stay out of the sun as much as possible.

- If you get lost in a heavily wooded area and you have read the first part of this book, you will know how to start a fire. Clear an area and light your fire. When it's going well and you have enough firewood to keep it going all night, repeat your efforts and build two more just like it. A single fire is an indicator that someone is camping at your location. Three fires, preferably set in a triangle shape, is an old time distress signal...it's just like writing SOS in big letters, and it makes you much easier to spot from the air.

- If your car breaks down far from civilization, stay with your vehicle. A vehicle can provide shelter from the elements and there are all sorts of items you can find inside one that might help you survive. When the search starts for you, the car will be easier to spot than you will. A roadway will be searched long before the searchers start looking in the trackless wilderness, it's a matter of logic.

- Surviving a plane crash, regardless of the size of the craft, is a miraculous occurrence. Keep your head, evaluate your situation, collect the items you can find to help you survive until the searchers find you, and *stay with the aircraft*! They will spot the wreckage and the debris from the crash far more quickly than they will spot your body in the wild.

- Don't rely on just your fires to attract the attention of search aircraft. Find a reflective surface, preferably a mirror, and try to signal passing ships, planes, or vehicles. A three inch mirror can generate a signal that can be seen from as far away as two and a half miles. Remember to focus the mirror in the direction of any vehicle, land, air, or sea, that you can see. If you have trouble aiming at a specific object or vehicle, break off a forked branch and use it as you would a gunsight to focus your reflection in the proper direction. While you're looking for a search vehicle, find any available glass that you can't use for anything else and break it into pieces, scattering it all around you. The people searching for you from the air will be able to see the reflections off the glass, and if you are forced to leave the site, scattering the glass in open areas exposed to sunlight will give them a trail to follow.

- If you should ever encounter a bear in the wild, your response is going to be determined by what kind of bear you've confronted.

- Grizzly bears tend to respond with aggression to humans in motion. Getting down in a fetal position and appearing as dead and defenseless as possible is your best option, but be aware that bears in general are unpredictable. You should also be aware that bears in general can outrun and outclimb just about anyone. Staying passive is your best defense short of possessing a really large and powerful weapon. Black bears have more of a tendency towards avoiding trouble. Your best bet with a black bear is to be aggressive and loud. If one gets too close, punch it in its sensitive nose. Once again, absent you possessing a large and powerful gun, there's little else you can do. Remember not to confuse the two. There's an old saying that deals with bears; "If brown get down. If black yell back."

- Cougars are another matter entirely. Playing dead in front of a cougar is like issuing him an engraved invitation to dinner. Cougars are not bashful at all about eating carrion, they are big animals and it takes a lot of fuel to run their bodies, especially in the wild when there's a lot of competition for food. Use anything at hand, such as a blanket, a sleeping bag, or a rucksack to make yourself appear larger and act aggressively. Be loud. If you're having a good day these things will scare him off.
- If you ever have the misfortune of being impaled or stabbed, don't try to remove the penetrating object. Its presence in the wound is helping to stanch the free flow of blood.
- Tampons are an excellent substitute for sterile dressings. They are sterile, and they are incredibly absorbent. What a survival tool!

- We're back to tampons again! Far from being an attempt at juvenile humor, the ubiquitous feminine hygiene products are virtual gold in a survival kit! As strange as that sounds, it's not even a remotely sarcastic. A tampon is comprised of four parts: an airtight wrapper, string, cotton wadding, and a plastic tube. You can make an expedient fishing bobber by opening the wrapper at one end, removing the tampon, and then tying the wrapper closed with a bubble of air trapped inside. If you can't get it to float, reopen the wrapper and place some of the cotton wadding inside the bubble. Once it's floatable, you can tie your bobber to your fishing line.
- We're not done with tampons yet! The wadding will make absolutely ideal tinder for starting a fire.
- Tampons appear to be the gift that keeps on giving. Pack the plastic tube with the cotton wadding and use it as a filter straw for drinking sediment-laden water.
- The string from a tampon can be used to tie a puff of the cotton wadding to the end of whatever you find to use as a shaft for a dart to use in the blowgun the piece of plastic tubing has become.
- When you get stung by a wasp or a bee, don't attempt to pull the stinger out. When you squeeze the stinger, you compress the venom

sac, injecting more venom into your skin. You should scrape the stingers out with the blade of a knife or with your fingernails. This can be a critical decision if you're allergic to bee stings. Anaphylactic shock is not a pleasant experience.

- One thing is a virtual certainty anywhere in the world except in a desert…you can almost always find a body of water somewhere nearby. If you have the proper knowledge, water means food, but if fishing is not in your repertoire of skillsets you could be in a real bind. Of course, if you're reading this, you'll have a ready solution. Surprisingly, if you are wearing a shirt and you're not so dehydrated that you can't spit, you have all the equipment you need to catch small fish and minnows! Untuck your shirt from your pants and wade into the water, lifting the front of your shirt to form an improvised net just under the surface of the water. Then you simply spit in the water. Fish will be attracted to the spit because they perceive it as food. When they gather in front of you, lift your shirt up out of the water and get ready to eat. You can cook up your catch as a crunchy goulash or a soup, you can use it as bait to catch bigger fish, or you can split your catch and do both.

- You can make a lens out of ice to make a fire. Break out a chunk of ice and shave it with a knife to get the rough shape of a lens. If a knife is not handy, grind your chunk of ice on cement or on a stone. Complete the fire lens by using the warmth of your hands to melt the ice smooth. The larger the lens is, the better it will collect sunlight. The lens needs to be about two inches thick and roughly six inches in diameter. Make certain the lens is smoothly curved on both sides. Then use the lens to light your tinder the same way you would use a magnifying glass.

- You can get an accurate compass bearing easily with a simple analog watch. Hold the watch horizontally and orient it so that the hour hand is facing towards the sun. The center point between the twelve and the hour hand will be your north/south line, with north being the direction indicated by the center line axis facing away from the sun. If the hour hand is pointing at four, the two would be oriented towards the south and the eight would be oriented towards the north.

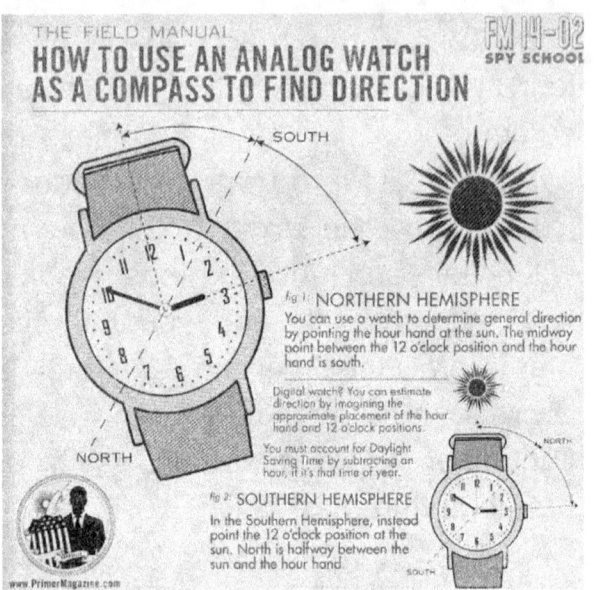

www.primermagazine.com

- This only works in the Northern Hemisphere, and if you're on Daylight Savings Time you would need to use the one instead of the twelve to determine the center line. In the Southern Hemisphere, orient the twelve towards the sun, and the north/south line will be indicated cut directly between the twelve and the hour hand, and north will be closest to the sun.

- Did you know that you could build a rudimentary metal detector with a handheld radio and a pocket calculator? You can! Select the AM band on your portable radio and tune it to any frequency that doesn't pick up a station, the higher the frequency the better. The only sound you hear should be static. Turn up the volume, and pick up your calculator (It should be turned on) with your free hand and hold them near each other at an angle until you hear a loud tone. Then carefully move them apart until the tone is just a loud buzz. (I just watched a video on Youtube.com that showed the radio and calculator affixed to a CD case so that the correct angle and distance could be easily maintained!) When you have the proper and have achieved the light buzz, you can sweep the device over the ground and any metal buried fairly close to the surface cause the sound to grow stronger.

- Most people will die of dehydration after three or four days without water, though there are documented cases of people lasting a week, but it would be unwise in the extreme to count on it. Absent any other source, you can always extract water directly from the ground. A solar still, a construct that utilizes a tarp or a sheet of plastic to collect evaporated water from dirt, can be easily manufactured. Dig a hole in the ground in direct sunlight. The size of the hole will be determined by the size of the material you have to drape over it. For the best results, dig where the vegetation is thickest and greenest. Place a cup or a can, something to catch the condensed water, in the center of the hole. Then drape your plastic (a tarp will work, but a sheet of soft plastic such as Saran Wrap is best) over the hole and seal the edges with logs, rocks, or, better yet, with the dirt you have removed from the hole. Place a small stone or pebble directly in the center of the cover so that your cover forms an inverted cone terminating directly above your collection container.

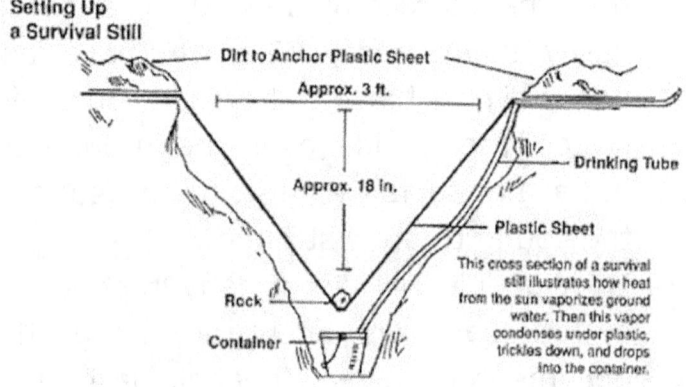

Setting Up a Survival Still

oldglorygunsmith.blogspot.com

- When the sunlight strikes the cover, the air trapped inside the hole heats up and the moisture in the dirt begins to evaporate. As the moisture is released from the earth, it will condense on the underside of the cover and run to the lowest point before dripping into your container. This is a slow method to be sure, but you can speed it up a little by placing fresh vegetation loosely inside the hole before emplacing the cover.
- You can collect water from a heavy dew. Attach a clean rag to your ankles and walk

around through the grass in the early morning. The rag will absorb water and then be squeezed out of the rag and into a container. The process can be repeated until you have enough water to drink.

- The Dakota Fire hole is a great way to build and keep a fire in very windy conditions.

tnoutdoorforum.com

- The fire hole is basically two pits dug into the ground very short distance apart and connected by a tunnel. Start your fire in one pit, and the other pit acts as a chimney, drawing air, and therefore oxygen inside to fuel the flames. This is also an ideal way to keep a fire going in windy conditions, and it's also a great way to conceal the fire if you do not wish to be seen.

- First Aid for a lung puncture, a type of wound that penetrates through the chest wall and into the lung (sucking chest wound,) calls for sealing off the opening so that the chest cavity around the lung doesn't get more air pressure than the lung itself. When that condition occurs, the lung will collapse. Sucking chest wounds are generally fatal unless they can be treated immediately. In such an emergency a sheet of soft plastic, such as Saran Wrap, can be used to seal the opening and stop the flow of air into the wound. You need to leave an opening at the bottom of the covering so that air can leave through the wound without entering it. You might want to think twice before throwing away that sandwich wrapper!

- If you're outside in the cold, and entering into the first stages of hypothermia, that silly bubble wrap you love so much to play with could save your life. The air bubbles in the packing material establish an insulating shield that keeps body heat from escaping (dead air space is the very best insulation,) and the plastic outside keeps the ambient air from leaching heat from you as well as keeping you dry. For maintaining body warmth, bubble wrap is about seventy percent as effective as three cotton blankets.

- Here's another wild one that never crossed my mind. Who would believe that a condom could actually save your life? It's true, condoms can help you acquire food, water, fire, and shelter—the four basic necessities. To begin with, condoms make serviceable water storage containers. Condoms can expand to very large dimensions, and two or three of them can hold enough water for an individual for a week. They can also be used to start fires, as latex will ignite instantly, making it perfect tinder for starting a fire. Latex is impervious to water, and can be used to keep both tinder and matches dry under wet conditions. Condoms can be used as ties to hold a poncho or sheet plastic in place for a shelter, and they can also be used as the rubbers (no pun intended) for a slingshot. Who would have thought that a condom could provide you with supper?

- Tobacco has develop a horrible reputation over the last fifty years or so. That being said, a cigarette can be very beneficial at times. The tobacco inside can be ingested to remove parasites from your system. The nicotine in tobacco can relieve the pain of a toothache by simply holding it over the affected tooth, and it can also be used as an antiseptic and general pain reliever. Cigarettes can also be shredded for tinder and used to start your fire.

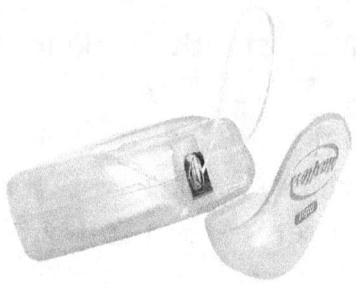

- **Dental Floss**
- Dental floss is another unexpected survival treasure. It can be used to make fishing line, used as tinder for fire starting, and it can be used to make a snare for small game. Held between two hands and used with a sawing motion, dental floss can be used to cut meats and vegetables. It can also be used as lashing to attach fletching to arrows and to make repairs to torn clothing. The carrying container for your dental floss can be used to store dry matches and tinder.

- Here's another sleeper! Steel wool can be used as tinder to create a fire, a small spark can easily ignite the steel wool. When very fine steel wool is separated or fluffed out, it can be easily ignited by touching both posts of a nine volt battery to it, *even if the steel wool is soaked in water at the time!*

- Steel Wool

- Extolling the virtues of Duct Tape would be an endless task. It can be used to repair just about anything, from patching a hole in your tent to mending your shoes. It can be used to make weapons, construct shelters, and even make mechanical repairs. I once used the stuff to mend a radiator hose on my 1964 Triumph TR-4 and subsequently forgot that I had done so. The duct tape covered hose lasted for several months before I realized what I had done and replaced it...but the hose was still working fine when I installed the new replacement. The miraculous stuff can be used to make shoes and clothing waterproof and hold dressings in place over wounds.

- • **Gaffer Tape**
- • A mini pry bar is a useful tool that takes up very little space in a survival kit, and it can be used for opening doors and windows, breaking up dry wood into kindling, and as a weapon for self-defense.

- • **Mini Pry Bar**
- • Animal Repellents can be used as a substitute for pepper spray, which requires a license to purchase in many states. Wasp spray can be an effective defensive weapon, and it can be used from much farther away than pepper spray, which makes especially versatile. Dog Repellent can be used to disorient and confuse an attacker and facilitate your escape.

Dog Repellant

- Pocket lint makes a very satisfactory tinder for starting a fire. You probably weren't really aware that you carry around highly flammable materials every time you put on your favorite jeans. When you need to light a fire very quickly and don't have a supply of tinder at hand, simply reach into your pocket and pull out some lint!   Lint is highly flammable and has a very low flash point.

- Ordinary household bleach can be used to purify water for drinking. A few drops can actually purify water and kill off any microorganisms present. This method of water purification allows us see or smell how well the bleach has killed the microorganisms and tells us when the water is ready to drink...but it takes a while. Fresh household chlorine bleach typically has about 5.35% chlorine and you should read the label before using it to ensure that you don't use too much chlorine for purification. Add two drops of bleach to each quart of water and then stir it well. Let the solution sit for half an hour before drinking it. If there are suspended particles in it and the water appears cloudy, start over with untreated water and strain it through a soft clean cloth or other acceptable filter. Try again adding four drops of bleach to each quart of water and then stir and wait for it to settle.

- Thompson Water Seal is a wonderful waterproofing agent. It can be used on many different fabrics to keep them from leaking. You need to be careful however, and remember to test the product on a small area before smearing it all over the outside of your tent. After it dries, check to see that it did in fact waterproof your item.

- Once your mind accepts the concept of creating a stove from a tin can there are as many variations on the original concept as there are people who think about it. A tin can stove is perfect when you need to cook something but can't stop to create a large fire. The basic concept is to find a fairly thick walled can with an open top, and then you make holes in the sides to allow for the entrance of oxygen to the heating chamber. The fire can be fueled by compressed Trioxane tablets we discussed earlier, by gel type fuel such as Sterno, by a homemade gel type fuel you can mix yourself using laundry detergent and gasoline, by candles, or by alcohol. The tin can stove is very efficient and can bring a cup sized container of water to a full boil very quickly. Larger cans may be constructed to cook with larger pans and fueled the same way. The sky is the limit with these stoves and you are limited only by your inventiveness.

- Anyone with military service has fond memories of a little device that was supplied along with C-Rations. The legendary P-38 can opener was often kept on a service member's dogtags so that it wouldn't get lost. Millions of these tiny useful tools now adorn keychains or languish in jewelry boxes as cherished mementos of days gone by. That isn't to say that they aren't still useful. Once you master their use (that usually involves some sore fingers) you can open cans of any size rapidly and efficiently.
- You can start a fire with reflected and focused light even if you don't have a magnifying glass or a piece of ice. Rubbing chocolate onto the bottom of a can, especially one of the aluminum cans with a concave bottom, you can create a brilliant, glossy shine. You use the glossy surface to focus the light on your tinder

and create flame in the same manner as you did with the magnifying glass.

- Ultra violet rays can literally burn your eyes. The symptoms may not show up right away, but they could appear unexpectedly at a later time, leaving you blind and unable to find your way home. If you don't have eye protection, bark sunglasses save your eyesight. Construction of bark sunglasses is very simple. Cut the bark into a shape that feels comfortable on your face and extends far enough to cover your eyes. Measure the distance between the pupils of your eyes and mark it off on the piece of bark. Bore a small opening over each mark, ensuring that the hole is roughly an eighth of an inch wide at most. Cut a wedge shaped piece for the bridge of your nose out of the bottom center of your bark. A string, a strip of cloth, or whatever is available can be used to secure them on your head. Snow goggles can be made from whatever materials are close at hand, and whatever is easiest for you to work with.

REFERENCES:

U.S. Army Survival Manual: FM 21-76

U.S. Army Ranger Handbook: SH 21-76

U.S. Army Field Manual: 3-05.70 Survival

U.S Army Field Manual: FM 8-5 Medical Field Manual

U.S. Army Field Manual: FM 4-25.11 First Aid